IF I ONLY HAD A HEART

Bridge over the rainbow

Alex Adamson & Harry Smith

LEO·9

D1321339

Master Point Press • Toronto, Canada

To our very patient wives,
Elinor Adamson and Alison Smith

Master Point Press
214 Merton St. Suite 205
Toronto, Ontario, Canada
M4S 1A6   (647)956-4933
Email: info@masterpointpress.com
Websites: www.masterpointpress.com
                 www.teachbridge.com
                 www.bridgeblogging.com
                 www.ebooksbridge.com

Library and Archives Canada Cataloguing in Publication
Adamson, Alex, author
     If I only had a heart : bridge over the rainbow / Alex Adamson and Harry Smith.
Short stories.
Issued in print and electronic formats.
ISBN   978-1-77140-035-0   (paperback).--ISBN   978-1-55494-632-7 (pdf).--
ISBN 978-1-55494-677-8 (html).--ISBN 978-1-77140-876-9 (html)
     1. Contract bridge--Fiction. I. Title.
PR6101.D368I3 2016   823'.92   C2016-905429-2
                                                 C2016-905430-6

Editor   Ray Lee
Copyeditor/Interior format   Sally Sparrow
Cover and interior design   Olena S. Sullivan/New Mediatrix

1 2 3 4 5 6 7   19 18 17 16
PRINTED IN CANADA

Preface

I have known Alex for more than thirty years. For part of this period, we were a regular partnership playing in most of the main Scottish tournaments and also traveling farther afield to events in Europe. We still play together occasionally.

We have discovered during that time a lot of interests in common both in the world of bridge and also more widely. We have similar views on many issues and similar tastes. In particular, we both read bridge literature avidly, keen to improve our own game. Through this wide reading, we each came across the genre of humorous bridge writing from the early days of S.J. Simon to the modern day, with its zenith in the wonderful works of Victor Mollo.

Over the decades, individually we have written bridge articles for magazines and newspapers. Many were serious, but some were humorous. We discussed the idea of a joint venture, and then Alex showed me an idea he had been working on for some time using characters from L. Frank Baum's *The Wizard of Oz*. We both thought the idea had mileage, but it was clear a lot of work was needed.

Then we were interrupted. I was appointed captain of the Scottish Senior Team at the 2012 European Championships in Dublin. When we won the bronze medal, we qualified automatically for the World Championships in Bali the following year. This was a major event in Scottish bridge. Scotland had been sending its own national team to major events since 2000, but had had no success whatsoever. There was huge interest in our forthcoming participation among the world's greats.

I decided to maintain a blog while I was in Bali. Alex and I discussed this and agreed that when I returned, we would see whether this could be developed into a book. The result was *Scotland's Senior Moment*, and with help from Brian Senior and Ray Lee, this was published in the summer of 2014.

Writing that book confirmed a number of things. First, we enjoyed working together. Second, it produced a better result than writing separately. We were forthright and frank in our appraisal of each other's work and, very importantly, neither of us minded being on the receiving end. The result was that no chapter in this or the previous book can be ascribed to either one of us. All are joint efforts and the result of much toing and froing.

We started producing the stories in this book as stand-alone articles shortly after we finished working on *Scotland's Senior Moment*, and by early 2015, we had about half a dozen ready and a number more in the pipeline. We approached Mark Horton with them and were delighted when he and the editorial board of *Bridge Magazine* decided to publish them. From the middle of 2015, they have been a regular feature in this journal, and in 2016 they began appearing in *Australian Bridge*.

Along the way, Ray Lee of Master Point Press, who had given us so much encouragement while producing the previous book, took an interest, and the result is that we are now able to offer to a wider audience the exploits of Dorothy, the Tin Man, the Lion, the Scarecrow, and so many others as they go through a year of playing bridge in the Over the Rainbow Bridge Club.

We hope you enjoy the result.

Harry Smith
Scone, Scotland
September 2016

Contents

Prologue

Every town in every country in the civilized world has a bridge club. Every bridge club has its own distinctive character, and many a tale could be written about each one. There is a club, however, that stands out above all others, one where the unusual is the norm. A club whose membership contains a number of characters who would try the well-known patience and tolerance of any bridge club committee.

The Over the Rainbow Bridge Club has an interesting and unusual history, having been created by the merger of two long-standing clubs that had found it financially beneficial to share the same premises. Some years later, a full union was achieved over the dead bodies of certain individuals on both sides.

The cultural difference between the former clubs was heightened by one being a men's club, the Lollipop Guild, and the other a ladies' one, the Lullaby League. To be fair, most members welcomed the union, as it brought more opportunities for finding a partner worthy of their talents. The last bastion of opposition came from a group of married couples (generally one from each "partnership") who saw their last reason for being unable to play with their spouse callously kicked from under them. Dorothy's Auntie Em had been one such person, or perhaps it had been her Uncle Henry — with the passage of time, it was something on which they were unable to agree.

Like every other bridge club, the Over the Rainbow Bridge Club has its own set of events, with many quirks and peculiarities. Some players believe that the events could be better organized and that the committee should be doing a far better job — not, of course, that they would consider joining it themselves, as that would remove one of the pleasures of membership: sniping from the sidelines. One thing they know for sure is that their Club is far superior, in some undefined way, to those round about, and especially to those in the country's capital, Emerald City, a well-known hotbed of people with an inflated view of their own importance.

tin man   SCARECROW   dorothy

LION

auntie em   uncle henry

hank   hickory   zeke

wicked witch
of the
west

IRRItaBLe witch

unpleasant
witch

Glinda

the
WIZARD

honorary chairman
of the
LOLLIpop GuilD

cissy

mayor of
munchkinland

ada

shy the
munchkin

Dorothy is one of the most popular members of the Club, despite her relative youth. She gets on well with all the members with whom this is possible. She is a good player, though perhaps not as technically proficient and logically incisive as her regular partner. His coldness and heartless insensitivity have earned him the nickname of the Tin Man. He speaks disparagingly of the lesser members of the Club. Many of these people actually have names, and indeed Dorothy knows most of them, a fact that is lost upon her partner as superficial and irrelevant. Most members consider the Tin Man to be the best player in the Club, something he is willing to confirm if asked.

Resplendent in a thick mane of hair and much admired by the lesser members of the Club (at least, those who do not check the scores) is a gentleman known to all as the Lion. He has a veneer of confidence, exuding bonhomie to all, but when he comes up against the better players, his courage often fails him. Partly to cover up his failings and partly to show up well in comparison, his regular partner is undeniably one of the worst players in the Club. With his unkempt, straw-colored hair growing out of his head and ears at all angles, he is generally known as the Scarecrow. Though he knows that he is lacking in the brains department, he is constantly trying to improve himself and feels honored and reassured by the presence of the Lion opposite him.

Dorothy, the Tin Man, the Lion and the Scarecrow often play together as a team in various Club events, achieving a fair degree of success. One of their main opponents is a group of ladies who live outside the town, at the four points of the compass. In this team, the strongest personality and best bridge player is a most unpleasant character known as the Wicked Witch of the West.

She takes great pride in being malevolent and can find a reason for antipathy towards men, women, old, young, tall, short, blonde, brunette... indeed everyone. Dorothy attracted her ire more than twenty years ago simply by moving to the town, buying a house in the east end that the Wicked Witch's sister had expressed interest in. For reasons unexplained, the sister has not yet been able to find a suitable property in the area.

The Wicked Witch's teammates are two other obnoxious characters, christened by the Tin Man as the Irritable Witch of the South and the Unpleasant Witch of the North. They are a well-matched partnership. Both enjoy creating chaos at the table, upsetting opponents and each other. They each bid with the primary aim of ensuring that the hand is right-sided, which means their partner lays down dummy. The Wicked Witch struggles to keep partners but is often to be seen playing with the glamorous Glinda: beautiful, well-dressed, successful in business, pleasant to everyone, she has everything going for her — apart from bridge ability. As a contrast to her teammates, she is known as the Good Witch.

Living on a farm outside town are Dorothy's Auntie Em and Uncle Henry, among the few surviving stalwarts of the two original clubs. Em is a dangerous opponent: her bidding lacks sophistication but not aggression. She has an excellent nose for the game and plays the hands well. Her direct style applies to conversation as much as bidding. Uncle Henry is, by necessity, less talkative and knows that he is not in her class as a bridge player.

Part of the duties of their farm workers is to make up a four in the farmhouse and in the Club's team events. The best players among the farmhands are Hickory and Zeke. Hickory is very able in all aspects of the game. Indeed, he is so good that Auntie Em respects him — not a common occurrence. Zeke is a good card player but likes to ensure he makes his contracts. This leads him into competition with the Lion for the title of the Club's worst underbidder.

There are many other players of varying degrees of competence in this very successful Club. Now and again a visitor will appear; the local rule is that such a player is considered a shark until proven innocent.

1

Trῡe or False?

Like most bridge clubs, the Over the Rainbow Bridge Club holds its main championship at the end of the season. Unlike other bridge clubs, the Over the Rainbow Bridge Club doesn't know when its season ends.

When the Lollipop Guild and Lullaby League Bridge clubs united thirty years ago, this proved to be something of a tricky issue, as they ran to different calendars. The men of the Guild had for some decades met in a golf club. The ball and stick game had to take precedence in the summer months, and bridge was allowed to come to the fore again as fall took hold. They had considered May as the end of their season.

The ladies of the League had met in a church hall, which was out of bounds to them during December and early January, as it was required for a sprinkling of festive events such as the nativity play and the pantomime (Auntie Em's Aladdin is still talked about today, with growing incredulity). They had followed the formal rather than the sporting year and had considered November to be its conclusion.

The new committee considered various options. At one stage, the idea of running the championships in February or August, exactly halfway between the two dates, was receiving a lot of support. Neither side would lose face: the two dates were equally unsuitable to both sets of members.

Attractive as this made it, compromise was never an option for certain members of each of the previous clubs. So the Over the Rainbow Bridge Club now has two club championships. One runs on Mondays from September to May with each pair counting their best twelve scores. The other takes place on four Fridays in November, with two nights of qualifying and two for the final and consolation events.

This November, two results from the qualifying rounds stood out. Last year's winners, Dorothy and the Tin Man, had won by a distance with scores of 63 percent and 69 percent. This surprised no one, except for the Tin Man — he was disgusted with their opening effort, which was so low as to be within the reach of many players in the Club on their best days. On the other hand, the Lion and the Scarecrow had somehow sneaked into the final with a miraculous average of 52 percent. The latter were also last year's winners, but of the consolation event. The main final was new ground for the Scarecrow, a disheveled man whose brain seemed equally disordered. He was delighted to make it into the big league. He attributed their success to the number of bridge books he had read since the previous year, combined with the confidence exuded by his partner.

Truth be told, the Lion, for all his bluster, was a coward at heart and would have felt happier as a moderately big fish in the shallower pond. However, he acknowledged his partner's compliment, his large mane of hair bouncing up and down. "King of the table — that's me! Oh dear, I see we are starting against the stars tonight. Let's see if we can't bring them back to earth with a bump."

He gulped back his fear, and then noticed that the Scarecrow had a book hanging out of his pocket. "Falsecards by Mike Lawrence," he read, and winced.

"Oh, it's very good. I'll be looking for opportunities to use them tonight," the Scarecrow enthused.

The Lion whipped it out and put it under the leg of a wobbly table. "Yes, very useful, indeed. I'd really prefer you to concentrate on playing true cards. Believe me, you are a natural when it comes to the false ones."

A few minutes later, they were seated and ready to begin, the Lion and the Scarecrow sitting East and West, respectively, while the Tin Man had the South seat.

"Strong notrump, five-card majors," barked the Lion.

"Weak notrump, four-card majors," replied Dorothy.

Dealer West. N/S vul.

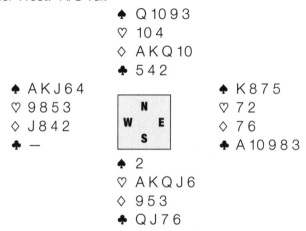

They waited for the Scarecrow to bid. After a couple of minutes, the Lion snorted. "You do know it's you, don't you?" The Scarecrow turned red, stammered something indistinct, and opened One Spade.

"Thinking about the last hand, I expect," suggested the Tin Man, a tall angular fellow with a voice like a rusty gate and personality to match.

Dorothy passed and the Lion bid Two Spades. The Tin Man elected to bid Three Hearts rather than double. After some thought, Dorothy raised to Four Hearts.

It had been a short auction:

West	North	East	South
Scarecrow	*Dorothy*	*Lion*	*Tin Man*
1♠	pass	2♠	3♡
pass	4♡	all pass	

The Scarecrow led the ♠A.

"Looks like Three Notrump might have been better," commented Dorothy, laying down dummy.

After collecting the first trick, the Scarecrow switched to a trump. The Tin Man won it in dummy and played a further three rounds, on which both dummy and the Lion parted with a club and a spade.

The Tin Man now turned his attention to clubs. Entering dummy with a top diamond, he led a club to his queen. The Scarecrow reached out to discard a small spade. Then a look of horror came over his face. Closer inspection of his ♠K revealed it to have what could only be described as clubbish tendencies. Quickly, he placed it on the table. There seemed nothing to do but play back a diamond.

The Tin Man went up with the king and played another club. The Lion rose with the ace, and the Scarecrow (after examining his cards carefully) threw a spade. The Lion continued with the ♣10, won by declarer's jack, while both the Scarecrow and dummy shed spades. With three tricks to go declarer needed the rest. This was the position:

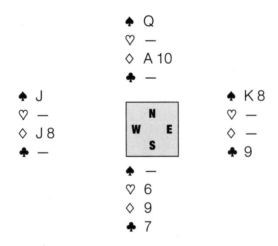

The Tin Man tabled his hand and pushed the ♡6 into the middle. "The defense has made the situation crystal clear. Let us consider the missing cards: to wit, three spades, two diamonds, and one club. The club is known to be in the Lion's hand. There are three spades yet to be played. Clearly, from the bidding and lead, the Scarecrow has king and another and the Lion has the last one. That being the case, the diamonds are split one each. What, you may ask, if the Scarecrow has all three outstanding spades and the Lion a club and two diamonds? Clearly, this is very unlikely, since nobody would voluntarily raise the Scarecrow on a doubleton. Even so, this presents no problem. I will play my last heart. The Lion, in order to hold onto his last club, will have to discard one of his diamonds."

The Tin Man was now in an exuberant mood. "You were quite right, partner: Three Notrump would have been easier, but even our friends here couldn't fail to take their four top tricks. I fancy our 620 will score very well."

He paused to accept their surrender. The Lion's eyes glowed angrily. "I'm sure you're right, as usual, but would you mind playing it out?"

The Scarecrow threw the ♣J, and both dummy and the Lion followed suit, throwing spades. The Tin Man next played the ◇9, to which the Scarecrow followed with the eight.

"The Scarecrow's last card is the king of spades," said the Tin Man, "and so the jack of diamonds is about to fall. Play the ace, partner."

Dorothy did so, and the Lion, with his chest puffed out, detached the ♠K from his hand, slowly lowered it towards the table, and with a look of contempt at the Tin Man, turned it over.

"I think the last one is mine," said the Scarecrow, revealing the ◇J. He looked apologetically round the table. "I'm terribly sorry I didn't have the king of spades. I can see why you thought I had it — I thought so myself to start with, and then when I realized it was my bid, I felt I had better say something in case you thought I had been thinking."

The Lion chuckled. "Don't worry, partner, no one would have accused you of that. Misplacing your king was a fine bit of falsecarding."

The Tin Man started to splutter. Dorothy tried to calm him down.

"Don't worry about it," she said. "It's just one hand. There's a long way to go." She put the next board on the table:

Dealer North. Both vul.

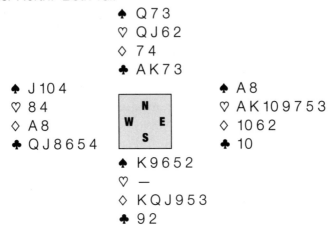

```
                    ♠ Q 7 3
                    ♡ Q J 6 2
                    ◇ 7 4
                    ♣ A K 7 3
   ♠ J 10 4                          ♠ A 8
   ♡ 8 4              N              ♡ A K 10 9 7 5 3
   ◇ A 8          W       E          ◇ 10 6 2
   ♣ Q J 8 6 5 4       S            ♣ 10
                    ♠ K 9 6 5 2
                    ♡ —
                    ◇ K Q J 9 5 3
                    ♣ 9 2
```

West	North	East	South
Scarecrow	*Dorothy*	*Lion*	*Tin Man*
	1NT	2♡	3♠
pass	4♠	all pass	

As dealer, Dorothy opened a weak notrump and the Lion overcalled Two Hearts. Still feeling annoyed by the previous board, the Tin Man jumped to Three Spades. Dorothy raised to Four Spades. Even if Three Notrump was the right contract, this was not the moment to suppress support for the Tin Man's suit. That ended the auction and the Scarecrow had to find a lead.

The Scarecrow was feeling ecstatic. He wasn't used to being complimented. Clearly, his book on falsecarding had done the trick. He carefully selected the ♡4.

The Tin Man gave his usual grunt when dummy appeared. Dorothy had long since come to accept it as a substitute for "thank you, partner." The Tin Man was actually quite pleased with what he saw. If he could hold his losses to two trumps and a diamond, or vice versa, he would be all right. The lead was covered by the jack and king, and the Tin Man ruffed.

He was unsure as to the best line. It seemed to depend on the location of the three missing aces. He could rely on the Lion being sound, perhaps even ridiculously over-sound, for his bidding. Dorothy's Auntie Em never allowed the Lion to forget the time she had opened Two Clubs on a hand the Lion had judged to be worth a weak two. Admittedly, the Lion had lost one of his aces on that occasion and thought he had only a 14-count. On the current hand he could be relied upon to have at least two of the aces and could have all three.

There was the possibility of a diamond ruff to be considered, should either opponent hold four. Also, he wanted to lose the first defensive trick to East to protect his heart holding. All in all, it seemed best to try and take some trumps out — with luck, East would have the ace. Catering for a singleton or doubleton ♠A in the Lion's hand, the Tin Man crossed to the dummy with a club and led a trump to his king and then one back towards dummy. The Scarecrow's ten was ducked and the Lion had to win the ace. As the Lion contemplated his next move, the Scarecrow led the ◊8.

"Lead out of turn!" cried the Tin Man.

The Scarecrow looked bewildered. "But you played low from the dummy under my ten of spades...."

"You may not have reached that page in your book," the Tin Man replied in his most caustic voice, "but your partner's ace beats your ten." He quickly considered his options: if the eight was a singleton, he could prevent an immediate ruff. "As a regular partner of the Scarecrow, Lion, I'm sure you're well aware of the rules for leads out of turn. I forbid you from leading a diamond."

These were the remaining cards:

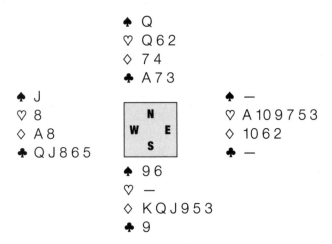

```
                  ♠ Q
                  ♡ Q 6 2
                  ◊ 7 4
                  ♣ A 7 3
  ♠ J                              ♠ —
  ♡ 8              N               ♡ A 10 9 7 5 3
  ◊ A 8       W         E          ◊ 10 6 2
  ♣ Q J 8 6 5      S               ♣ —
                  ♠ 9 6
                  ♡ —
                  ◊ K Q J 9 5 3
                  ♣ 9
```

With a snarl, the Lion thumped the ♡A on the table. The Tin
Man nonchalantly threw a diamond and turned to the Lion,
nodding with approval at the Scarecrow's eight, confirming
clearly that he had started with three hearts. His contract was
now almost assured. He would win the enforced heart or club
return in the dummy, pull the outstanding trump, and play on
diamonds. That Scarecrow's misplay of the ◊8 would be very
costly to him. It was now very likely, the Tin Man thought to
himself, that the Scarecrow had started with a singleton or
small doubleton in diamonds. To a player of the Tin Man's
caliber, finessing the ◊9 was obvious.

"You're still on lead, so you're still forbidden from leading
a diamond," the Tin Man announced, acid dripping from each
word. The Lion continued with another heart, on which the
Tin Man threw another diamond. Checking carefully that he
wasn't revoking, and that he had correctly identified the trump
suit, the Scarecrow ruffed with the ♠J and cashed the ◊A, taking the contract one down.

"Bad luck, partner," said Dorothy. "Without the lead out
of turn, I am sure you would have made it. The heart force
wasn't an obvious defense. Say it goes a diamond to the ace
and a heart back; you ruff and play diamonds. Whenever the
Scarecrow chooses to ruff, you can overruff and return to hand
by trumping a club or heart."

The Tin Man gasped, as if winded. "I can see that," he said, "but how was I to know this idiot," he pointed to his left, "would lead low from a doubleton not just once but twice?" He turned on the Scarecrow. "The opening lead I can almost understand. After all, these spots can be tricky to count. But what, pray, were the thought processes behind your switch to the eight from ace eight doubleton — if the word 'thought' has any meaning at all in the context of your play?"

"Well," began the Scarecrow, blushing, "you see, my book says that when the defense can see no legitimate way of beating a contract, they should try and mislead declarer in the hope that he will go wrong. You looked so confident and I honestly had no idea how to defeat you, so I thought I would try a little subterfuge." He looked up at the Lion. "I'm terribly sorry, partner. I seem to have messed it up again. Would it have gone down more if I hadn't led out of turn?"

The Lion purred. "On the contrary, partner, it was another well-judged falsecard. Perhaps I'll take a look at that book after all."

 # The Master Play

The Club Pairs' Championships had reached the final night. The Tin Man was not in a good mood.

"We're lying third," he said, glaring at Dorothy. "Third, in this field of Munchkins!"

"How many times do I have to tell you that pairs can be like that," said Dorothy, trying desperately to calm him down before play started. "You can't legislate to stop idiocies working occasionally. And when you play that Scarecrow, you can guarantee some idiocies will happen."

"It's a matter of dignity," the Tin Man announced in his most grating metallic tones. "I am without doubt the best player here, and you may well be the second best. For us not to retain this trophy would be like a women's team winning the Spingold."

"And why shouldn't a women's team be able to win the Spingold?" Dorothy's face tingled as her blood pressure rose.

"Oh, now you are just being ridiculous," said the Tin Man dismissively.

How can I get him to calm down? Dorothy wondered. Fortunately, just at that moment, the director called for play to start.

Three hours later, as the last move was called, the Tin Man was still not happy. "We're winning tonight, of course," he whispered to Dorothy as they moved to their new seats, "but I'm not sure we're winning by enough to overtake both these pairs of cretins who were ahead of us. Fortunately, we have just the right opponents for this last round." His face actually moved into a semblance of a smile as he took the North seat with the Lion coming to his left and the Scarecrow to his right.

"Aaargh!" roared the Lion as he strode up to the table, "Three easy tops coming for us, Scarecrow!"

"You've got a nerve," Dorothy said, laughing. "Oh — I was forgetting you lost it years ago."

The Lion whimpered indistinctly as the Tin Man glared at him in his usual unfriendly fashion.

This was the first hand:

Dealer East. N/S vul.

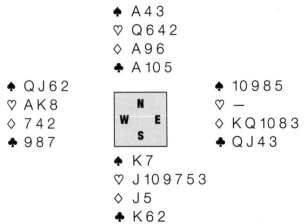

```
                    ♠ A 4 3
                    ♡ Q 6 4 2
                    ◇ A 9 6
                    ♣ A 10 5
  ♠ Q J 6 2                        ♠ 10 9 8 5
  ♡ A K 8          N              ♡ —
  ◇ 7 4 2     W         E         ◇ K Q 10 8 3
  ♣ 9 8 7          S              ♣ Q J 4 3
                    ♠ K 7
                    ♡ J 10 9 7 5 3
                    ◇ J 5
                    ♣ K 6 2
```

After three passes, the Tin Man opened a weak notrump on the North cards. The Lion and the Scarecrow didn't play any special defense to One Notrump, so the Lion was able to overcall a natural Two Diamonds. Dorothy bid Two Hearts and the Scarecrow raised to Three Diamonds. The Tin Man raised Dorothy to Three Hearts. The Lion passed quickly. He had bid on 8 points, and his partner, a passed hand, had raised him to the three-level. Thank goodness the opposition had come to his rescue, and he wouldn't have to play the hand.

Dorothy looked at her hand. She knew she should pass, but surely the Scarecrow on lead was worth a trick. Yes! She bid Four Hearts, which ended the bidding. The full auction was:

West	North	East	South
Scarecrow	*Tin Man*	*Lion*	*Dorothy*
		pass	pass
pass	1NT	2◊	2♡
3◊	3♡	pass	4♡
all pass			

The Scarecrow dutifully led a MUD ◊4, and Dorothy surveyed her prospects. Nine tricks seemed routine, and she would probably need a little help from her friends to make a tenth. Still, there was always hope.

She won the ◊A and played a trump, won by the Scarecrow's king. He played back the ◊7. The Lion won and, seeing no further hope in that suit, switched to the ♠10. Dorothy took that in hand and played another trump. The Scarecrow won his second high trump. He knew from many years of criticism that as he was unlikely to find the best defense himself, it was always the safest policy to try to follow his partner's defense. At least it led to less criticism. He returned the ♠Q. Dorothy won the ace and played two more rounds of trumps, ending in hand. At this stage, declarer had lost two trumps and a diamond, and these were the remaining cards:

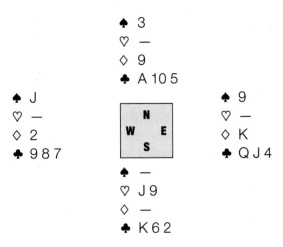

```
              ♠ 3
              ♡ —
              ◇ 9
              ♣ A 10 5
  ♠ J                      ♠ 9
  ♡ —         N            ♡ —
  ◇ 2     W     E          ◇ K
  ♣ 9 8 7      S           ♣ Q J 4
              ♠ —
              ♡ J 9
              ◇ —
              ♣ K 6 2
```

On the next heart, the Scarecrow threw away his last diamond, dummy threw a club, and the spotlight fell on the Lion. Trusting that his partner had the ♣J, he threw his nine so as to keep hold of the minors. On the last heart, the Scarecrow was squeezed in the black suits. He had to throw away a club to stop dummy's ♠3 becoming a winner. That card having done its work, Dorothy pitched it from the dummy. Now it was the Lion's turn to feel the pinch. He clutched first the ♣4, then the ◇K, then went back to the club. With a snarl, he tossed it onto the table. With the remaining clubs now 2-2, Dorothy had the last three tricks. The Tin Man grabbed the traveling score sheet. Dorothy's +620 was a clear top.

"There was nothing we could do, partner," the Lion said, shrugging. "We just happen to have been sitting against the only declarer up to playing the double squeeze."

The Tin Man was ecstatic. This pair were the perfect opponents to have with such tight scoring. There were still two boards to go. He might as well put the boot in!

He turned to the Lion. "On the contrary, it is more likely that you were the only defenders to set up a double squeeze against yourselves. It's obvious to anyone with a grain of intelligence that if either of you plays a third round of diamonds early on, the squeeze is obliterated.

"Even without taking that simple precaution, you could have saved yourself at the end. When defending a double squeeze, it is a general rule that you try to guard the suits held on your right. When the penultimate trump is played, you must keep hold of your spade, trusting that partner has 9xx or better in clubs. If he hasn't, then the last trump is going to squeeze you in the minors anyway. Throwing a club from your hand will mean that on the last trump, the Scarecrow will be able to throw his spade (not that I'm saying he will) and keep his three clubs. Whether a spade or a diamond is thrown from the dummy, you will be able to do the same in comfort. Declarer will be left with a loser however she plays it."

There was a stony silence as they started the second board. It turned out to be a very simple deal. The Scarecrow became declarer in Three Notrump and carefully timed the play to make nine of his ten top tricks. The Tin Man was jubilant. Another board like one of these two, and they would be a certainty for first place.

On the third and final board of the round, with both vulnerable, Dorothy held:

♠ J 9 6   ♡ Q 5   ◇ Q J 7   ♣ K Q J 10 4

On her left, the Scarecrow opened One Club and the Lion alerted. The Tin Man passed and the Lion bid One Heart.

"What was the One Club?" Dorothy inquired.

"Who knows with my partner," he bellowed. "It could be as much as nineteen or twenty points!"

"Behave." She glared at him. "You play five-card majors and a natural diamond, don't you?"

The Lion winced. He could never keep up his brazen exterior in front of Dorothy. "Um... er... yes, five-card majors and a... a... a... fifteen to seventeen notrump. So it's either natural or a balanced hand outside that range," he whimpered.

Dorothy passed and the Scarecrow raised to Two Hearts. That was passed back to Dorothy. Had the Scarecrow been playing the hand, she would probably have passed, as his incompetency at the helm would have almost ensured a good score. However, the Lion was moderately competent, so she decided it was better to try and push them up a level. She

bid Three Clubs and, sure enough, the Scarecrow bid Three
Hearts. Dorothy felt pleased, and then she noticed the Tin
Man thinking. Eventually he bid Four Clubs and everyone
passed. This was the auction:

West	North	East	South
Scarecrow	Tin Man	Lion	Dorothy
1♣	pass	1♡	pass
2♡	pass	pass	3♣
3♡	4♣	all pass	

The Scarecrow led the ♡A and dummy appeared:

> ♠ A Q 8 2
> ♡ 6 3
> ◇ K 9 3
> ♣ 9 8 7 6
>
> ▬▬▬▬▬
>
> ♠ J 9 6
> ♡ Q 5
> ◇ Q J 7
> ♣ K Q J 10 4

Not a pretty sight, but Dorothy remained polite as usual.
"Thank you, partner," she said with a gulp. She had four top
losers and then spades to think about. Meanwhile, though
Two Hearts looked safe, whether three would make was far
from clear.

After the ♡A, the Scarecrow switched to a small one, to the
Lion's king. The Lion switched to a trump, won by the Scarecrow's ace. Dorothy took the trump return, noting disappointedly that the Lion had followed suit so the opponents definitely
had a club loser. To help her place the remaining high cards,
she led the ◇J from hand. The Scarecrow went up with the
ace and played another heart. Thank goodness for that straw-
brained idiot, thought Dorothy, as she ruffed in the dummy
and threw a spade from hand.

Dorothy ran through the play so far. She was already one down. The Scarecrow had played three aces and the Lion had shown the ♡K. If the Scarecrow had the ♠K he had at least 15 points. Since he clearly had a balanced hand, and since the Lion's paw could use a few more points, it was obvious that the ♠K was on her right. That was good news in that it meant Three Hearts was making, but bad news in that it meant she was going to go two down, and -200 would be a very poor score. Thinking fast, she saw a chance to avoid a spade loser. She played the ♠A from the dummy and then a small one, hoping that the Lion wouldn't put up his king when she was "obviously" going to ruff it. The Lion played low worryingly quickly and the Scarecrow took her jack with the king. This was the full hand:

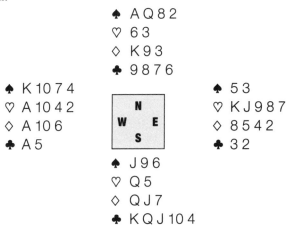

```
                    ♠ A Q 8 2
                    ♡ 6 3
                    ◇ K 9 3
                    ♣ 9 8 7 6
  ♠ K 10 7 4                        ♠ 5 3
  ♡ A 10 4 2          N             ♡ K J 9 8 7
  ◇ A 10 6        W       E         ◇ 8 5 4 2
  ♣ A 5               S             ♣ 3 2
                    ♠ J 9 6
                    ♡ Q 5
                    ◇ Q J 7
                    ♣ K Q J 10 4
```

"Why didn't you open One Notrump?" Dorothy asked the Scarecrow, trying to remain calm.

"Ah, that's because we play a fifteen to seventeen notrump, and I only had fourteen."

"You had three aces and a king!" said Dorothy.

"And three tens," added the Tin Man.

"Are you sure?" asked the Scarecrow. "I added them up twice. Mind you, it did seem an awfully good fourteen. That's why I went on to Three Hearts."

"I see you would only have gone one off if our avian-repelling friend hadn't given you that ruff and discard," said the Tin

Man, unfeelingly. "You would have had nothing to try but the double spade finesse. I just hope that two tops to us and one to them is sufficient."

The Scarecrow perked up. He had been responsible for them getting a top. The Tin Man had said so. That ruff and discard had been a master play. He resolved to do more of them.

It was an anxious wait for the Tin Man once play had finished. The thought of having to congratulate some Munchkin on winning a trophy that should clearly be his own was abhorrent to him. It was with considerable relief that he heard the director announce their success — relief so great that he never even noticed the indignity of winning by just 1 matchpoint.

2

The Phantom Menace

For two consecutive weeks, the Tin Man had finished below the Lion and there was no way that he was going to allow the run to extend to three. Dorothy was unperturbed, partly due to her more relaxed nature, and partly because she had been away on holiday when the unmentionable events had taken place. Indeed, she was rather amused by his discomfiture.

In the first week of her absence, the Tin Man had played with Dorothy's Uncle Henry, practicing for their upcoming outing together in the annual men versus ladies match. If the purpose of practice is to identify areas that need work, then it was a great success, giving the Tin Man an unaccustomed interest in the bottom quarter of the result sheet: 44.8 percent was not a good score in anyone's book, and even the Lion and the Scarecrow had been higher, with 49.2 percent.

In the second week, the Tin Man had played with the Mayor of Munchkinland. "Bumptious, self-important, and unwilling to listen to reason" was how each of them described their partner after the event. With the Scarecrow absent with a nasty head cold, the Lion had played with an adoring but only moderately competent Munchkin. Filled with courage by his partner's unquestioning confidence and helped by the absence of some of the stronger players, the Lion cut a swathe round the room. As hand after hand failed on unlucky breaks, the Lion's "sound" judgment was justified time and again as they powered to an unstoppable 65 percent.

Now Dorothy had returned and she stood in front of the notice board looking at the results of the previous few weeks. The Tin Man joined her.

"Sometimes one feels that the score would make more sense if it was the other way around," he observed. Dorothy decided not to mention that inverting the order would not have changed the Tin Man and the Mayor's position, coming as they had right in the middle of the field.

With the Scarecrow recovered, both regular partnerships were restored and they faced each other in the first round. The Tin Man and Dorothy sat North and South, respectively. The Lion was West and the Scarecrow, East.

Dealer South. Both vul.

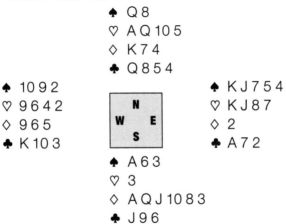

```
                    ♠ Q 8
                    ♡ A Q 10 5
                    ◇ K 7 4
                    ♣ Q 8 5 4
    ♠ 10 9 2                         ♠ K J 7 5 4
    ♡ 9 6 4 2          N             ♡ K J 8 7
    ◇ 9 6 5        W       E         ◇ 2
    ♣ K 10 3           S             ♣ A 7 2
                    ♠ A 6 3
                    ♡ 3
                    ◇ A Q J 10 8 3
                    ♣ J 9 6
```

As they sorted their cards, the Lion announced, "We are experimenting with weak notrump and four-card majors tonight."

"How brave of you," said the Tin Man. "We've been playing that for years."

"Well, perhaps you should have the courage to try something different once in a while," the Lion muttered.

Dorothy interrupted their discussion by opening One Diamond. The Tin Man responded with One Heart and the Scarecrow overcalled One Spade. Dorothy rebid Two Diamonds. The Tin Man felt Three Notrump was the most likely contract, but he wanted help in spades. He bid Two Spades. Dorothy obliged with Two Notrump and the Tin Man raised her to Three Notrump.

The Lion led the ♠10. Dorothy ducked twice, then won the ace on the third round. Obviously, she could take six diamond tricks and the ♡A to get to eight tricks. The heart finesse seemed unlikely to win, but there was no need to commit herself at this stage. She rattled off her diamonds and the Scarecrow felt himself under growing pressure. His first problem was that he wasn't entirely sure how many diamonds Dorothy had. He had been expecting five on the strength of her Two Diamond rebid. Perhaps it was a comment on Dorothy's declarer play that in her hands it felt like more. His first three discards weren't too painful. He could afford two small hearts and a club. That brought him down to:

$$\spadesuit\,J\,7\quad \heartsuit\,K\,J\quad \diamondsuit\,-\quad \clubsuit\,A\,7$$

For his fourth discard, the Scarecrow chose his second small club. The last diamond came as a nasty surprise. He felt that if he agonized, then threw the ♡J, Dorothy would be bound to drop his king. He threw one of his spade winners, hoping that Dorothy would try the heart finesse for her ninth trick. However, she read the position correctly, playing a club to his ace. He was able to take one spade trick, then had to lead into dummy's ♡AQ.

"Well played, though poorly bid," said the Tin Man.

Well, any compliment from him was worth getting, thought Dorothy, although she was at a loss to explain the criticism. "Go on then, explain," she said.

"What made you think the notrump contract would be better played from your side? If you bid Three Spades over my Two Spade cuebid, you will allow me to right-side the contract."

Meanwhile, the Lion had been considering the defense. "Aaargh! Bare your king of hearts early, as if you don't care about the suit. Then Dorothy might finesse to you, or if she tries to endplay you, you'll have the tricks to cash to beat her! You must plan your discards in advance in these situations!"

The Scarecrow blushed. He had no answer to that. The Tin Man, however, had.

"Why give declarer any chance to make the contract? Having scored two tricks at the start, the defense needs three more tricks to beat the contract. The sure way to do that is to keep losers and throw winners away!" He paused, waiting for them all to ask him to explain.

Dorothy, who had, after all, played the hand, did not need to. "What he means is that I can't make it if you throw away your spade winners. If you do, we will come down to…" she quickly scribbled down the position on the back of her score-card.

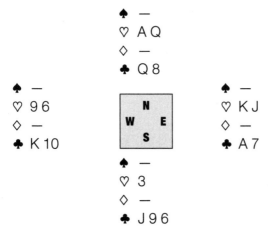

"Whatever I do, you will come to two club tricks and the king of hearts."

The Tin Man's chair creaked slightly as he shifted uncomfortably. "Quite so."

The Lion raised his eyes to the ceiling. "My partner's probably now made a mental note that he must, in future, throw winners away on the run of declarer's long suit. At least I can take comfort that he doesn't remember anything by the time he reaches the next table!"

They took out their cards for the second board. For ease of reading, the hand is rotated here ninety degrees, making the Scarecrow South.

Dealer South. Neither vul.

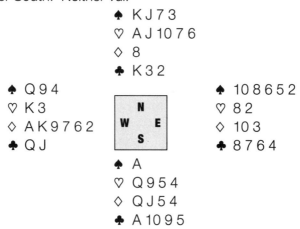

      ♠ K J 7 3
      ♡ A J 10 7 6
      ◇ 8
      ♣ K 3 2

♠ Q 9 4   ♠ 10 8 6 5 2
♡ K 3   ♡ 8 2
◇ A K 9 7 6 2   ◇ 10 3
♣ Q J   ♣ 8 7 6 4

      ♠ A
      ♡ Q 9 5 4
      ◇ Q J 5 4
      ♣ A 10 9 5

The Scarecrow looked at his hand with a feeling of pleasure — a chance to open a four-card major at last. He bid One Heart and Dorothy overcalled Two Diamonds. The Lion bid Two Spades. He intended to show his heart support later, if necessary. In the meantime, there was a chance that the Scarecrow would raise spades, right-siding the contract. If not, at least he would learn something more about his partner's hand.

The Tin Man passed and the Scarecrow had a problem. Since they were playing a weak notrump, he felt sure that a notrump rebid would promise a stronger hand. While Two Notrump seemed in many ways the most descriptive bid available to him, the Lion was sure to notice he was several points short. He had heard of something called "fast arrival." It was something to do with overbidding on a weak hand. That could be the solution to his problem. Seeing it as the least of all evils, he decided to rebid Three Notrump.

Something worrying then happened. The Lion went into a long trance and then emerged with Four Notrump. Perhaps the Lion hadn't heard of fast arrival? Perhaps one was supposed to bid Three Notrump more quickly to get the message across? This time the Scarecrow passed as rapidly as he could. In a state of shock and absolute panic, he prepared himself first to play the hand, and second for the onslaught that would surely follow at the end.

The auction had been:

West	North	East	South
Dorothy	*Lion*	*Tin Man*	*Scarecrow*
			1♡
2◊	2♠	pass	3NT
pass	4NT	all pass	

Dorothy led a small diamond and the Lion put his hand down with an angry growl. Even the Scarecrow could see that Four Hearts was secure and would even probably make eleven tricks if the heart finesse worked. Meanwhile, if it lost, then even Three Notrump might not make, let alone Four Notrump. He won the Tin Man's ten with his queen, took a deep breath, and placed the ♡Q on the table. That scored. A second round of hearts discovered the king, and the first hurdle had been overcome. The Scarecrow now had ten tricks but still probably a matchpoints bottom, unless people were going down in slam. He ran off his remaining hearts and noted that the Tin Man threw a spade, a club, and a diamond. He himself threw a diamond on the last heart. Dorothy threw three diamonds. They were now down to:

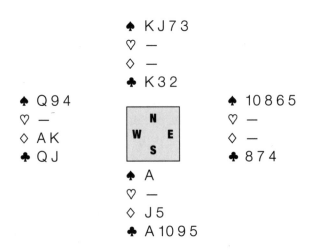

```
              ♠ K J 7 3
              ♡ —
              ◊ —
              ♣ K 3 2
♠ Q 9 4                      ♠ 10 8 6 5
♡ —          N              ♡ —
◊ A K      W   E            ◊ —
♣ Q J          S            ♣ 8 7 4
              ♠ A
              ♡ —
              ◊ J 5
              ♣ A 10 9 5
```

The Tin Man's club discard gave the Scarecrow some hope of extra tricks. He cashed the ♣K, then paused for breath when

Dorothy dropped the queen. This, he knew from his books, was a restricted choice situation. He would finesse the ♣9, cross to the ♠K, then repeat the finesse. Suddenly, he saw the fatal flaw in his logic — he had no small spade to lead to the king.

Ears burning with shame, he played a second club to the ace. When the jack dropped, the Scarecrow cashed the ♣10 and ♣9, expecting to concede two diamonds. However, Dorothy was having difficulty deciding what to discard. Clearly, the opposition bidding had gone badly wrong, but the Scarecrow had to have the ♠A to even have an opening bid. It was therefore essential to hold ♠Qxx as her last three cards. That would at least give the Scarecrow a choice as to whether to finesse or not at Trick 12. Hoping that the Tin Man held the ◇J, she threw the king and ace.

The Scarecrow looked in amazement. He was sure he had held the ◇Q earlier in this hand — or was it on the last one? Yes, it was this hand! How could a good player like Dorothy make such a silly error as this? He cashed the ◇J and noticed that no one else had any of that suit. That meant his ◇5 was also a winner. To his astonishment, he found he had won all thirteen tricks and scored a surprising +520. The Scarecrow felt very humble. He supposed that if he hadn't blocked the spades he could have made fourteen.

"Very good," came the Tin Man's grating voice. "How inventive to allow declarer to play that diamond suit for three tricks and no loser." Dorothy could tell that he would be irritable for the rest of the night and silently wished that she was back on holiday.

At the end of the session, the Lion was checking over the frequencies. His face brightened as he saw the scores for the second board.

"Nobody bid that slam," he announced. "It was a good job you made thirteen tricks, though. Two Wests went for 500 in diamond partscores, so you just pipped them." The Scarecrow and Lion left happy, with a healthy 54 percent — happier than Dorothy and the Tin Man with their 58 percent. Not content with having overcome the Lion, the Tin Man was now moaning about a third consecutive score below 60 percent.

3
The Battle of the Sexes

Back in the mists of time, when there had been two bridge clubs in town — one for men and one for women — financial constraints and common sense had pulled the two first under one roof and then into one club. The memory of these clubs was kept alive by the presence of wallboards listing the former presidents and champions up to the date of the union thirty years before. Nowadays, the only echo of these times past was the annual team of eight match between the sexes, playing under the names of the original clubs.

Dorothy's Auntie Em had been appointed captain of the Lullaby League team some years before — the details were sketchy and no one could quite remember what the mechanism had been, but her position was not disputed. Em had informed Dorothy that they would be playing together.

The Lollipop Guild still retained a position of Honorary Chairman. This personage chaired a committee that was comprised of himself, the Mayor of Munchkinland, and the Lion. The Chairman and the Mayor played together, and the Lion played, of course, with the Scarecrow. For the past three years, the Tin Man had formed an uncomfortable partnership with Dorothy's Uncle Henry for the match. After their recent, disastrous practice match, the Tin Man had taken the Honorary Chairman aside and expressed his doubts about their continued participation.

"Not at all, not at all," said the Chairman. "You are a vital member of our team and we would struggle to win without you. Besides that, Henry admires you so much, and looks forward to playing with you in the match: it is a special event for him and he feels honored to get to play with the best player in the club."

"Well, yes, I can see it being something of a treat for him, but we're not on the same wavelength at all, and he is so inflexible," protested the Tin Man. "Maybe we could both play, but with different partners?"

"Not at all, not at all," said the Chairman again. "I understand what you are saying about Henry. But who else could we pair him up with? Who would put up with his fixed ideas? Really it has to be you. I'm sure that you can see that."

The next morning the Chairman received a phone call from Uncle Henry, wanting to withdraw from the match.

"Not at all, not at all," said the Chairman. "You are a vital member of our team and we would struggle to win without you. Besides that, you have played on our team for over forty years — you are a link with the old club before the union. It wouldn't be the same without you, and I know that old Tinny feels honored to be your partner in this event. He was talking to me about it just yesterday."

"Well, yes, I can see it being something of an honor for him, but we're not on the same wavelength at all, and he is so inflexible," protested Henry. "Maybe we could both play but with different partners?"

"Not at all, not at all," said the Chairman. "I understand what you are saying about Tinny. But who else could we pair him up with? Who would put up with his fixed ideas? Really it has to be you. I'm sure that you can see that."

Egos suitably managed, the gentlemen of the Lollipop Guild assembled on the appointed night to take on Auntie Em's Lullaby League ladies. It would prove to be a match where unexpected cards beat, or had the potential to beat, contracts.

Auntie Em was a woman of few methods but made up in aggression what she lacked in sophistication. She took the North seat, while Dorothy sat South. They started against Zeke and Hickory, two of Em and Henry's farmhands who completed the Guild's eight. They picked up:

Dealer East. E/W vul.

```
                  ♠ 7 6
                  ♡ J 9 8 4 2
                  ◊ A K Q 5
                  ♣ Q 6
    ♠ 5 4 2                        ♠ Q J 10 9 8
    ♡ 5              N             ♡ A K 10 7 3
    ◊ 10 9 7 6 4   W   E           ◊ 2
    ♣ 10 9 5 4       S             ♣ 8 3
                  ♠ A K 3
                  ♡ Q 6
                  ◊ J 8 3
                  ♣ A K J 7 2
```

Zeke, sitting East, opened One Spade. Dorothy considered her hand too good to overcall One Notrump, so she started with a double. Hickory passed and Auntie Em cuebid Two Spades. Dorothy jumped to Three Notrump, hoping her aunt would read the strength of this correctly. Auntie Em did indeed, and seeing no good way of developing the auction, leapt to Six Notrump. East's double ended the auction.

West	North	East	South
Hickory	*Auntie Em*	*Zeke*	*Dorothy*
		1♠	dbl
pass	2♠	pass	3NT
pass	6NT	dbl	all pass

Hickory, in the West seat, was not at all sure what to lead. His brain did not feel at its sharpest after the previous night, when Auntie Em had been uncharacteristically generous with the whisky. If his partner had two aces, it probably didn't matter. It was far from impossible that he had the ♠AK or the ♠KQ and an outside ace. All things considered, it seemed safest to lead his partner's suit. His MUD ♠4 went to the eight and ace.

Dorothy looked forlornly at her eleven top tricks. It was hard to see where a twelfth would come from. It was unlikely that too many others would get to slam, so they seemed booked for a loss. Still, the best start would seem to be to run the clubs and see how things developed. East threw an encouraging ♡10, followed by the three on the third and fourth rounds of the suit, while dummy parted with two small hearts.

On the fifth club, West had to make a discard. Signaling was the part of the game Hickory enjoyed most. It seemed to him that his role in the hand was to give his partner as much information about the distribution as possible to allow him to hold on to the right cards to beat the contract. He carefully selected the ♠5 to show that his initial lead had not been top of a doubleton. Another heart was thrown from dummy and the ♠Q from East. Dorothy now started on diamonds. After three rounds of them, this was the position with the lead in dummy:

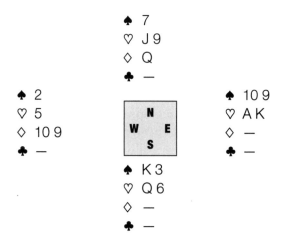

```
              ♠ 7
              ♡ J 9
              ◇ Q
              ♣ —
♠ 2                        ♠ 10 9
♡ 5          ┌──────┐      ♡ A K
◇ 10 9       │  N   │      ◇ —
♣ —          │W    E│      ♣ —
             │  S   │
             └──────┘
              ♠ K 3
              ♡ Q 6
              ◇ —
              ♣ —
```

Dorothy led the ◇Q from the dummy and Zeke, in the East seat, was squeezed. A heart discard would allow Dorothy to set up a trick in that suit. Hoping his partner had started with ♠5432, he pitched a spade. Dorothy threw one of her hearts and took the last two spade tricks for her contract.

"Sorry," said West. "It was a fairly hard lead to find."

"I can understand the lead," replied East, "but did you really have to squeeze me? It's not as if you had many big cards to hold on to. Could you not find room for the five of spades? If you had thrown a diamond and kept the five-two of spades then I could have thrown a spade, leaving you to guard them."

After an uneventful remainder of the round, the Tin Man and Uncle Henry arrived at Dorothy and Auntie Em's table for the next round. From their body language, Dorothy guessed that their wagon still retained most of its wheels. This was the first hand.

Dealer South. E/W vul.

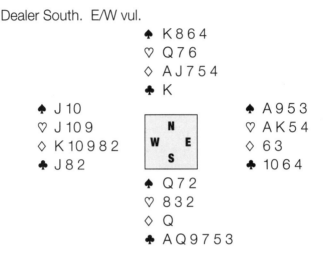

                    ♠ K 8 6 4
                    ♡ Q 7 6
                    ◇ A J 7 5 4
                    ♣ K

    ♠ J 10   ♠ A 9 5 3
    ♡ J 10 9   ♡ A K 5 4
    ◇ K 10 9 8 2   ◇ 6 3
    ♣ J 8 2   ♣ 10 6 4

                    ♠ Q 7 2
                    ♡ 8 3 2
                    ◇ Q
                    ♣ A Q 9 7 5 3

Dorothy, as South, knew her hand wasn't a classic three-level opening. However, the vulnerability was in her favor and the Tin Man and Uncle Henry were an inexperienced partnership; with any luck, they would not be clear what they were doing over preempts. Best of all, it would annoy the Tin Man. She decided to open Three Clubs.

As it turned out, it was Auntie Em who had been preempted. However, lacking a fit, she passed and Three Clubs became the final contract.

West	North	East	South
Tin Man	Auntie Em	Uncle H	Dorothy
			3♣
all pass			

The Tin Man, West, led the ♡J. Dorothy knew that he could not possibly have underled the ace-king, so she ducked in case they were doubleton on her right. The jack held and

Uncle Henry won the continuation. He took a third heart and switched to a trump. Dorothy won with the king in dummy and considered her prospects. With three hearts lost already, she needed trumps to split kindly and still had to avoid losing two spades. The diamonds might provide a discard, or the ♠A might be doubleton. In any case, she needed to get back to hand to try to draw trumps, and it seemed sensible to leave diamonds untouched — they might come in handy later. She led a low spade from the dummy and was pleased when the queen scored: the Tin Man's jack did not escape her attention. She cashed the ♣A and ♣Q and was relieved when they split 3-3.

Dorothy contemplated her next move. It was still possible that Uncle Henry as East had started with the doubleton ♠A, although the jack would have been a strange card for the Tin Man to play from ♠J109x. What if the Tin Man had a doubleton? If it was ♠J10, then life could be made difficult for the defense. However, she would first need to finesse the ◊Q. This passed off successfully, leaving these cards:

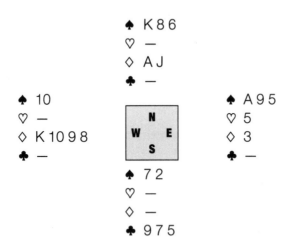

Dorothy played a low spade from hand. The Tin Man played the ten and Dorothy called for a small card from dummy. Uncle Henry could see that if he overtook with his ace, he would be setting up dummy's king for Dorothy's ninth trick, so he ducked. The Tin Man was no better placed. He had to play a diamond, giving Dorothy the chance to throw her last spade on dummy's ace.

"What an undisciplined bid," came the Tin Man's grating voice, "leading to a disgusting contract. It's just a pity that on the fortunate lie of the cards it stumbled home."

Mission accomplished, thought Dorothy, though she avoided saying anything.

Meanwhile, the Scarecrow and the Lion were sitting East-West against the Irritable Witch of the South and the Unpleasant Witch of the North. Again, South opened Three Clubs. The Lion as West passed; the Unpleasant Witch of the North thought for a few seconds, then passed, as did the Scarecrow. The Lion led the obvious ♡J.

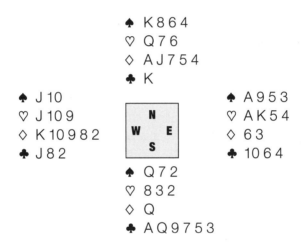

The Irritable Witch of the South scowled at her partner as she appraised the dummy. "What on earth were you thinking about?"

"Well, Three Notrump is not out of the question, even opposite one of your bat-eaten preempts," sniffed North unpleasantly.

"Three Notrump? With the bare king of clubs and no heart stopper? How did you plan to get to my hand — by broomstick?" squawked declarer irritably.

The Scarecrow's brain drifted during this exchange. He would not have bid Three Notrump with the North cards. For one thing, there was too much danger that he would end up playing the hand. Still, it was the sort of thing that the Tin Man did and it always seemed to work for him. He was brought back to the table by a low growl from his partner. He saw that declarer had played the ♥Q from the dummy. He won his king.

By now, the Scarecrow had forgotten what the real contract was and was defending the one being discussed. This was a rare pleasure, as he could see how to beat it. He cashed the ♥A, and when he saw his partner's ten, he began to have an uneasy feeling. He seemed to have blocked the suit. Fortunately, he had an entry. He could even pretend that it was all part of a clever plan to take an extra trick if his partner had the ♠QJ! He led back the ♥5, feeling rather clever to be giving a suit preference signal. South followed and the Lion won the nine. The Lion followed his partner's indicated defense, switching to the ♠J. The Scarecrow won the ace and with an air of satisfaction placed the ♥4 on the table.

The Irritable Witch of the South snarled at him and discarded the ♣9. The Lion discarded the ♣J, and, much to the Scarecrow's surprise, the ♣K was thrown from the dummy. As the Scarecrow considered this strange development, declarer called for a small spade from dummy. The Scarecrow looked questioningly round the table.

"But I won the last trick, I think."

The Unpleasant Witch of the North groaned. "Won it? You didn't even come third! Did you not notice any of the three ruffs?"

The Scarecrow felt lost, but he wasn't going to argue. He concentrated on following suit for the rest of the play. Declarer won in hand with the ♠Q, then laid down the ♣A and ♣Q. When the ten didn't appear, she conceded one down.

Declarer muttered an indistinct curse under her breath.

"So it seems I wasn't such a mad old bat after all!" crowed the Unpleasant Witch. "Three Notrump by me is cold and Three Clubs by you goes down."

"Cold?" shrieked the Irritable Witch. "So hearts 4-3 with the ace-king in the same hand, clubs 3-3 and the ace of spades on the right side is what qualifies as cold nowadays, is it?"

"I'm sorry," mumbled the Scarecrow. "I know it's wrong to give a ruff and discard. We were very lucky to beat it after that."

"Don't worry," purred the Lion. "Without the trump promotion, we could do nothing to stop the contract declarer was in. What you executed was a sort of safety play. It ensured we beat the contract whether it was the one they had actually bid or the one you thought they were in."

 # A Tale of Three Jacks

At half-time, the ladies of the Lullaby League had a lead of just 12 IMPs.

The Tin Man came up to Dorothy, intent on unburdening himself by sharing his thoughts on her uncle's inadequacies. He had barely started when Auntie Em slid herself between them with surprising speed.

"You're not telling her anything she doesn't already know," she told the Tin Man as she whisked Dorothy away. "No fraternizing with the enemy," she said sternly to Dorothy. "If they're not getting on, let them stew!" She directed the pair of them towards a table where the Lion and the Scarecrow were sitting and drinking coffee and lemonade, respectively. Sensing double standards, Dorothy drew breath to speak, but Em cut her off before she had uttered a syllable.

"They're not the enemy. This pair is our fifth column, and the best part is that they don't even know it. They will be coming to our table next. Let's see if we can sow some seeds of doubt...."

At the restart, the Tin Man and Uncle Henry found themselves up against the Unpleasant Witch of the North and the Irritable Witch of the South.

Dealer West. Neither vul.

```
                    ♠ A Q 5
                    ♡ A 10 4 3
                    ◇ 10 7 5
                    ♣ 8 7 3
     ♠ J 9 6 4                      ♠ K 3 2
     ♡ K 9 8          N             ♡ Q J 5
     ◇ A K 8 2    W       E         ◇ 9 6 4 3
     ♣ 5 4            S             ♣ J 9 2
                    ♠ 10 8 7
                    ♡ 7 6 2
                    ◇ Q J
                    ♣ A K Q 10 6
```

After three passes the Irritable Witch of the South had the choice of opening One Club or throwing the hand in. She opted for the former. The Tin Man, sitting West, doubled, and the Unpleasant Witch of the North redoubled. Uncle Henry bid One Diamond, which was passed back to North, who competed with Two Clubs. After two further passes, the Tin Man competed, in turn, with Two Diamonds.

Double dummy, the limit of the hand had been reached with Two Clubs a safe make and Two Diamonds booked for one down on decent defense. The Irritable Witch, however, was in a quandary. If she bid on, she would be playing the hand, but on the other hand, if she passed, Uncle Henry would be at the helm, and that could be to their advantage. In the end, the thought of defending, which meant, after all, working cooperatively with her partner, was just unacceptable, and she bid on to Three Clubs. That concluded a green card dominated auction.

West	North	East	South
Tin Man	*Unpleasant*	*Uncle H*	*Irritable*
pass	pass	pass	1♣
dbl	redbl	1◇	pass
pass	2♣	pass	pass
2◇	pass	pass	3♣
all pass			

The Tin Man led the ◇A. Not wanting to lead away from his major-suit honors, he continued with the king and another diamond. Declarer threw a spade on dummy's winning ten and drew trumps in three rounds, leaving the following cards:

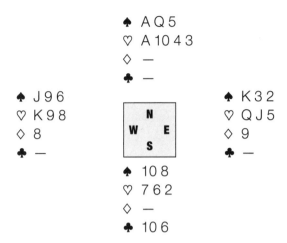

```
                    ♠ A Q 5
                    ♡ A 10 4 3
                    ◇ —
                    ♣ —
  ♠ J 9 6                          ♠ K 3 2
  ♡ K 9 8            N             ♡ Q J 5
  ◇ 8           W         E        ◇ 9
  ♣ —                S             ♣ —
                    ♠ 10 8
                    ♡ 7 6 2
                    ◇ —
                    ♣ 10 6
```

The Irritable Witch, as declarer, paused for thought. West, the Tin Man, had shown up with 7 points in diamonds, and having passed initially, he could not have both a high heart honor and the ♠K. There was no rush to take the spade finesse. If she could set up the fourth heart before a spade came through the ace-queen, she could use it to park her probably losing spade. That would give her five clubs, one diamond, two hearts, and a spade for nine tricks.

Hoping to duck a heart into Uncle Henry's hand she led low towards the dummy. The Tin Man had been using declarer's thinking time to assess the situation and played the king.

"Ace," said the Irritable Witch. Now the spotlight was on Uncle Henry. Seeing that he would have one safe exit in diamonds but would then be endplayed by the next heart if he kept both his honors, he placed the queen on the table with great care.

In a fit of pique that her plans had been seen though, the Irritable Witch grabbed the ♡3 from dummy and threw it into the middle of the table. Uncle Henry both disappointed her by not producing the jack and annoyed her by the melodramatic flourish with which he laid down the five. The trick was won by the Tin Man's eight. With a scathing glance to his right, he placed the ♠6 on the table. The contract was one down.

"Good defense, Henry," said the Tin Man.

"Yes, award-winning," the Unpleasant Witch of the North said, snorting. "An Oscar, perhaps."

The Lion and the Scarecrow were North-South on the same hand against Auntie Em and Dorothy.

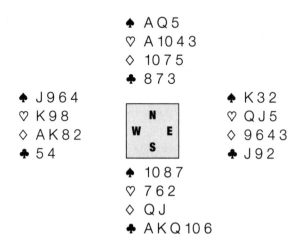

```
                    ♠ A Q 5
                    ♡ A 10 4 3
                    ◊ 10 7 5
                    ♣ 8 7 3
  ♠ J 9 6 4                          ♠ K 3 2
  ♡ K 9 8          N                 ♡ Q J 5
  ◊ A K 8 2      W   E               ◊ 9 6 4 3
  ♣ 5 4            S                 ♣ J 9 2
                    ♠ 10 8 7
                    ♡ 7 6 2
                    ◊ Q J
                    ♣ A K Q 10 6
```

The auction was essentially the same as at the Tin Man's table, leaving the Scarecrow to try his hand at Three Clubs. This was the sort of hand he liked to play. It was only likely to cost 4 IMPs if he went down and would barely rate a mention among all the double-figure losses he had caused. The defense started with three rounds of diamonds, and the Scarecrow managed just in time to stop himself from ruffing dummy's winning ten. He remembered seeing the ace, king, and queen but didn't know what had happened to the jack. Something funny seemed to have happened: he wasn't sure what and felt slightly unsettled. Trying to refocus, he turned his attention to trumps. He led out the ace, king and queen. He was aware that Auntie Em had shown out at some point, and again had managed to miss the jack. He tried the ten and was relieved when it scored, dummy pitching a spade and the defense their remaining diamonds. Without much of a plan in mind, the

Scarecrow played a heart. Auntie Em played the king and Dorothy emulated her uncle, though less dramatically, by putting the queen under the ace. They had come down to:

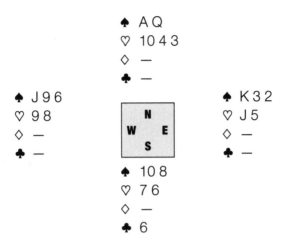

```
              ♠ A Q
              ♡ 10 4 3
              ◊ —
              ♣ —
♠ J 9 6                        ♠ K 3 2
♡ 9 8          ┌─────┐        ♡ J 5
◊ —            │  N  │        ◊ —
♣ —          W │     │ E      ♣ —
               │  S  │
               └─────┘
              ♠ 10 8
              ♡ 7 6
              ◊ —
              ♣ 6
```

The Scarecrow was enjoying this hand less and less. "Leave the cards up, please," he said. He had the distinct feeling that he was going to end up looking very foolish, as he seemed to have got every suit wrong so far. Having missed both minor-suit jacks, he had a strong feeling that he had now lost the ♡J, too. Nervously, he called for the ♡10 and sank back, deflated, in his seat when Dorothy won the trick with the jack.

But the defense was now helpless. Dorothy played a heart to Auntie Em's nine, and she played a spade back at top speed hoping to rattle the clearly distressed Scarecrow. Now totally confused and convinced that he could do no right, the Scarecrow called for the ace. He followed it up with the last heart, miraculously managed to discard his losing spade, and found after two recounts that he had made nine tricks.

Auntie Em rolled her eyes. "Perhaps now you can see why we used to have two clubs: to keep decent people away from that sort of performance."

On the final round, Auntie Em and Dorothy were North-South against the Mayor of Munchkinland and the Honorary Chairman of the Lollipop Guild.

Dorothy found herself looking at:

♠9　♡Q753　◇KQJ976　♣K7

With both sides vulnerable, Auntie Em opened One Heart. The Mayor overcalled Three Spades and Dorothy raised to Four Hearts. The Chairman's bid of Four Spades was passed back to Dorothy. Deciding that her second suit offered her good chances of making eleven tricks, she made a descriptive call of Five Diamonds. Auntie Em, being the sort of person who liked to take bids at face value, passed, as did both of the opponents. The full bidding had been:

West	North	East	South
Chairman	Auntie Em	Mayor	Dorothy
	1♡	3♠	4♡
4♠	pass	pass	5◇
all pass			

The Chairman led a small spade and dummy came down:

```
        ♠ Q
        ♡ A 6 4 2
        ◇ A 10 5 4
        ♣ A J 10 8
        ▭
        ♠ 9
        ♡ Q 7 5 3
        ◇ K Q J 9 7 6
        ♣ K 7
```

Well, at least Five Diamonds was a better contract than Five Hearts, thought Dorothy, though she might have to do some good guessing to get to eleven tricks.

The Mayor won the ♠K and switched to a trump. Dorothy won and took a second round, the Mayor discarding a spade. With the Mayor having shown, probably, eight cards in spades and diamonds and a preemptive hand, the Chairman was a favorite to hold the ♣Q, though it was odds against to be falling in three rounds. For the same reasons, the ♡K was very likely to be wrong, and hearts could easily be breaking badly. The hand was, in fact, much as Dorothy imagined:

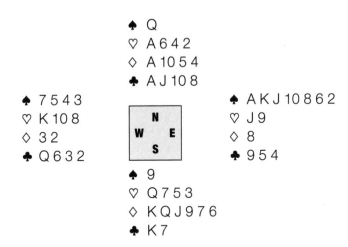

```
                    ♠ Q
                    ♡ A 6 4 2
                    ◊ A 10 5 4
                    ♣ A J 10 8
    ♠ 7 5 4 3                      ♠ A K J 10 8 6 2
    ♡ K 10 8          N            ♡ J 9
    ◊ 3 2         W       E        ◊ 8
    ♣ Q 6 3 2        S             ♣ 9 5 4
                    ♠ 9
                    ♡ Q 7 5 3
                    ◊ K Q J 9 7 6
                    ♣ K 7
```

Deciding that she would bank on the club finesse, Dorothy counted ten tricks. If the Chairman held the ♣Q and the ♡K, it might be possible to put him under some pressure, but only if she rectified the count. She decided to duck a heart, giving her squeeze chances as well as the possibility of dropping a doubleton king. When the Mayor won the ♡9 they were down to:

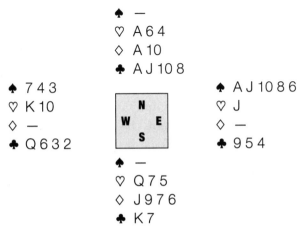

```
                    ♠ —
                    ♡ A 6 4
                    ◊ A 10
                    ♣ A J 10 8
    ♠ 7 4 3                        ♠ A J 10 8 6
    ♡ K 10           N             ♡ J
    ◊ —          W       E         ◊ —
    ♣ Q 6 3 2        S             ♣ 9 5 4
                    ♠ —
                    ♡ Q 7 5
                    ◊ J 9 7 6
                    ♣ K 7
```

Hoping to scramble Dorothy's entries, the Mayor played back a club but she hadn't come this far to fail. She rose with the king, cashed dummy's ♡A and rattled off her trumps. The first three rounds caused little pain. With one trump to go, this was the position:

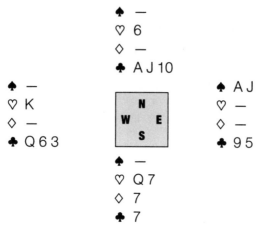

```
              ♠ —
              ♡ 6
              ◇ —
              ♣ A J 10
♠ —                           ♠ A J
♡ K                           ♡ —
◇ —                           ◇ —
♣ Q 6 3                       ♣ 9 5
              ♠ —
              ♡ Q 7
              ◇ 7
              ♣ 7
```

West had found it easy to discard his spades, but had no good answer to the last diamond. With an air of despondency he threw a club, allowing Dorothy to pick up the whole suit and throw both of her hearts.

"Well done, Dorothy," said Auntie Em as they walked over to score up with their teammates. "I just hope the rest of the girls haven't let us down." She quickly learned that she had nothing to worry about, as the women had scored well in the second half and recaptured the trophy by more than 30 IMPs.

The teams were called together and the Honorary Chairman stretched himself up to his full four feet two inches.

"I represent the Lollipop Guild, the Lollipop Guild, the Lollipop Guild," he intoned formally, "and on behalf of the Lollipop Guild, I wish to present the Lullaby League with the Union Cup. And thank you for a friendly and pleasant game."

"Friendly be damned," muttered Auntie Em to Dorothy. "And as for Union — what has been united can always be split apart. Still, at least this way I can see what your Uncle Henry is getting up to."

4

If I Only Had a Heart

"To be quite honest, I am still baffled by the whole concept," the Tin Man said for the third time. "What is a 'social' match, and what is the point of it? Am I not always sociable?" The Lion turned to stare at the Tin Man.

"Eyes on the road," said Dorothy.

The Tin Man continued. "Was I supposed to play badly? When I bid a vulnerable game, which I expected to make, and they sacrificed not-vulnerable, was I not supposed to double? Or was I supposed to concede the rest when we had already taken the contract for 1100 and I could squeeze her for 1400, then endplay her for 1700? I thought she would appreciate the beauty of my defense."

"That was not the problem, as I have already told you," replied Dorothy through gritted teeth. "No one likes to be told that their worst hand of the season will be immortalized in an article in the district magazine."

"I said I would hide the names."

"You also said that you would have to improve their bidding and her play, as there could be children reading."

"That was a joke! True, of course, but any improvements would be to avoid my incisive defense being clouded by the enormity of their inadequacies."

"Yes," said the Scarecrow. "'The enormity of their inadequacies.' That was the phrase I heard her repeating to the tournament director."

The four friends were returning from a friendly match between the Over the Rainbow Bridge Club and their equivalents from Poppyfield, a sleepy town on the main road to the Emerald City.

The match was played between teams of eight. The Over the Rainbow team had traveled in two cars. The match over, Dorothy, the Tin Man, and the Scarecrow were with the Lion in his large, powerful, gold-colored car, hurtling back home up the motorway at speeds approaching fifty miles per hour.

"I also do not understand," persisted the Tin Man, "why we did not stay for the buffet. I thought that socializing was supposed to be one of the key elements of this bizarre event. Apart from anything else, I thought that was where part of our table money went."

Dorothy refused to be drawn on this subject. "If you must write an article — " she began.

"Oh I must, I promised!"

"If you must," she went on, "then there were a number of other hands that are worth writing up. There were these two hands where you've explained in detail to each of us just how well you played them. They might be a more instructive read than the 1700 hand. It's important that you let people see just how well normal contracts can be played, rather than focusing on the defense against a ridiculous one." Dorothy hoped that if an article was unstoppable, then perhaps flattery could deflect it onto a less harmful path.

The match had been played through a Saturday afternoon with each pair playing four sets of six boards against the pairs in the other team. Each team had two North-South and two East-West pairs. The first eleven boards had been uneventful. This was the last board of the second set.

Dealer East. Both vul.

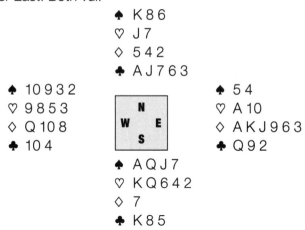

$\spadesuit$ K 8 6
$\heartsuit$ J 7
$\diamondsuit$ 5 4 2
$\clubsuit$ A J 7 6 3

$\spadesuit$ 10 9 3 2
$\heartsuit$ 9 8 5 3
$\diamondsuit$ Q 10 8
$\clubsuit$ 10 4

$\spadesuit$ 5 4
$\heartsuit$ A 10
$\diamondsuit$ A K J 9 6 3
$\clubsuit$ Q 9 2

$\spadesuit$ A Q J 7
$\heartsuit$ K Q 6 4 2
$\diamondsuit$ 7
$\clubsuit$ K 8 5

For the Over the Rainbow team, the Lion and the Tin Man were both sitting South. The auction at the Lion's table was over quickly. After a One Diamond opening from East, the Lion had doubled. West had passed and the Scarecrow had jumped to Three Clubs. East, rather boldly, had come back in with Three Diamonds. That had ended matters, though the Lion had felt a twinge of concern that they might have a 5-3 heart fit.

West	North	East	South
	Scarecrow		*Lion*
		1◊	dbl
pass	3♣	3◊	all pass

The defense had not gone well. The Lion had led his partner's suit, and after winning the ♣A, the Scarecrow had returned a low club to the Lion's king. The Lion now tried the ♡K, ducked all round. Has declarer played the ten holding ♡AJ10, hoping he would continue? he thought. Well, he's in for a shock if he has! He led his ♡Q, expecting his partner to ruff and giving the clear message that a spade return would get his partner a second ruff.

Events did not quite materialize as the Lion had hoped, the trumps providing an entry to the now established ♡98 for declarer to discard both spade losers. Fortunately, the Tin Man was so pleased with his own play on the hand that he hadn't bothered to ask how East-West had made ten tricks in diamonds with five seemingly unavoidable losers.

The auction was quite different at the Tin Man and Dorothy's table, where they were playing against two ladies with almost luminous pink rinses.

```
                    ♠ K 8 6
                    ♡ J 7
                    ◊ 5 4 2
                    ♣ A J 7 6 3
  ♠ 10 9 3 2                          ♠ 5 4
  ♡ 9 8 5 3          N                ♡ A 10
  ◊ Q 10 8        W      E            ◊ A K J 9 6 3
  ♣ 10 4             S                ♣ Q 9 2
                    ♠ A Q J 7
                    ♡ K Q 6 4 2
                    ◊ 7
                    ♣ K 8 5
```

West	North	East	South
	Dorothy		Tin Man
		1NT	dbl
redbl	pass	2◊	dbl
pass	3♣	pass	3♡
pass	4♡	all pass	

Over East's off-center strong One Notrump, the Tin Man had doubled for penalties. West's redouble was for rescue, showing a hand that was either a club one-suiter or a two-suited hand without clubs. East was expected to bid Two Clubs, so her Two Diamond rebid strongly suggested a six-card suit. The Tin Man's second double was for takeout. Dorothy's bid of Three Clubs showed values, and the Tin Man felt he had to press on for game. Over Three Hearts, Dorothy was in an awkward position. Four Hearts seemed to be the least bad option.

West led the ◊Q and followed that up with a second round. The Tin Man ruffed. The auction had been quite revealing. Unless West was messing around on a 4-3-3-3 hand it seemed very likely that she was 4-4 in the majors. Unless East's One Notrump was an out-and-out psyche, then she had to have all the remaining points, including the ♣Q.

If hearts were 3-3, then he could draw trumps and take four hearts, four spades and two clubs for ten tricks. If they were 4-2, then it would seem he had two hearts, a diamond and a club to lose. He played a heart to the jack and East's ace. East continued with a third diamond, forcing him to ruff again. He had been reduced to two trumps in hand, and when he played them, East followed to the first but then discarded a diamond.

West now had the only remaining trump, but the Tin Man was unperturbed. He led out his four spade winners and two club winners, safe in the knowledge that West would have to follow suit throughout. At Trick 13, he played his third club triumphantly and watched West ruff East's queen.

"I had four inescapable losers, as I hope you have observed," said the Tin Man. "I am delighted to be able to lose two of them on the same trick."

The lady in the West seat snorted. "Lucky lie. Still, I suppose there was nothing else for you to play for."

"I beg your pardon," stuttered the Tin Man. "I knew exactly what was going on in the hand."

"So then you will know exactly how lucky you were!" West smiled at him as she got up to move to the next table.

In the third quarter, Dorothy and the Tin Man were up against the Poppyfield Club Captain, and his partner, the Secretary. They found that the concentration of power in as few partnerships as possible made for greatly improved decision making.

Dorothy knew that their opponents were a decent pair and capable of putting up stiff resistance. After a couple of quiet boards, they took out their cards for this deal:

Dealer South. Both vul.

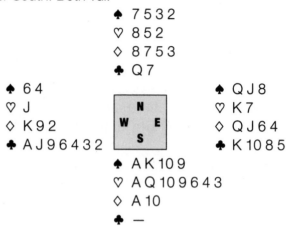

```
                    ♠ 7 5 3 2
                    ♡ 8 5 2
                    ◇ 8 7 5 3
                    ♣ Q 7
  ♠ 6 4                              ♠ Q J 8
  ♡ J                    N           ♡ K 7
  ◇ K 9 2           W         E      ◇ Q J 6 4
  ♣ A J 9 6 4 3 2         S          ♣ K 10 8 5
                    ♠ A K 10 9
                    ♡ A Q 10 9 6 4 3
                    ◇ A 10
                    ♣ —
```

The Tin Man opened the South hand One Heart. He heard a Three Club weak jump overcall on his left by the Captain, a pass from his partner, and Three Notrump on his right. He doubled. After two passes, the Secretary went into a huddle, emerging eventually with a jump to Five Clubs. The Tin Man doubled that too, and the Captain passed. The key decision now lay with Dorothy.

It seemed to her that every time she held a virtual bust, the Tin Man managed to put her on the spot. These opponents were not dummies, so it was unlikely that there was a big score coming from Five Clubs doubled. She had no way of knowing if it was even going down. She bid a reluctant Five Hearts, which was passed out. No double, no trouble, thought Dorothy.

The auction had been:

West	North	East	South
Captain	*Dorothy*	*Secretary*	*Tin Man*
			1♡
3♣	pass	3NT	dbl
pass	pass	5♣	dbl
pass	5♡	all pass	

The Captain led the ♣A. The Tin Man considered the dummy. He could see that they had been taking at best 500 from Five Clubs while Four Hearts was very likely to be making. Could he make his five-level contract, though? On the face of it, given that the Three Notrump bid seemed to rule out a singleton ♡K, he was booked to lose at least a diamond, a heart, and a spade.

He ruffed the opening lead with the ♡6, then played off ace and another diamond. The Captain, on his left, hesitated when playing low on the ◇10. The Secretary won the trick with the jack and played back a third round of the suit. The Tin Man ruffed this with the nine, while the Captain dropped the king. With the defense having already scored one trick, this was the position:

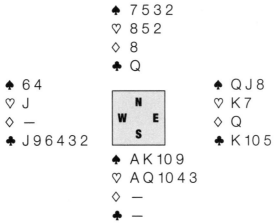

                ♠ 7 5 3 2
                ♡ 8 5 2
                ◇ 8
                ♣ Q
    ♠ 6 4   ♠ Q J 8
    ♡ J   ♡ K 7
    ◇ —   ◇ Q
    ♣ J 9 6 4 3 2   ♣ K 10 5
                ♠ A K 10 9
                ♡ A Q 10 4 3
                ◇ —
                ♣ —

Clearly, the Captain's store of high cards was almost exhausted. Virtually all the remainder were obviously with the Secretary, including the guarded ♡K. There were so many finesses that the Tin Man wanted to take by leading from the dummy, but so few entries to get there. Assuming that trumps were indeed 2-1, two top trumps would establish one entry, but that was not going to be enough — the Secretary was sure to put in a spade honor when he led one from the dummy.

In a moment of inspiration (or as he himself described it, genius), the Tin Man saw the answer. There was one realistic holding that would give him the contract, so he played for it. Giving the Secretary a meaningful look, he placed the ♡Q on the table. The jack fell on his left, dummy gave up its two, and the Secretary, with a light shrug of his shoulders, took the king. He tried a fourth diamond, but the Tin Man ruffed in with the ten. The Tin Man now played one of his carefully preserved small trumps to the eight, drawing the defense's last one, and called for a spade. He tabled his cards.

"I am going to play the double finesse. I will re-enter dummy with the five of hearts to repeat it. If you have both spade honors, Mr. Secretary, then I have my contract."

The opponents both considered this for a moment then conceded. "Well played — a pretty ending."

"Thank you — if Trick 5 can be called an 'ending,'" said the Tin Man. "And thank you again, for allowing me to play it."

"Well, Six Clubs was going for 800."

"Oh, no. I mean for pulling three notrump. I would have been endplayed at Trick 1 and forced to give you an eighth trick. A much better score for you. I suppose 'endings' don't come any further from the end than that!"

The Captain and the Secretary felt that, for them, the end could not come soon enough.

As they sat in the car on the way home, Dorothy reflected back on those happy times when her partner had only *irritated* the opponents — before the painful events of the last round.

They sat in their own thoughts for some time. The Tin Man fell asleep. Ahead of them, the lights of the town began to twinkle.

"You know," said the Scarecrow, breaking the silence. "It's funny, but it always seems to take less time to come back than it does on the journey out."

"Oh, indeed. It's a scientific fact," said the Lion in his most knowledgeable tones. "It's called the Law of Diminishing Returns."

Dorothy studied his face without success for signs that he was joking. She drew breath to speak, then exhaled, closed her eyes, and relaxed back into her seat.

5

D⊮mb and D⊮mber

The Club had been hit badly by the winter flu virus. Attendance was down and this had led to some unusual partnerships being formed.

The Lion had been one of the victims. Well, at least he had decided he was. He had sneezed once two weeks previously and had spent the fortnight since then in bed, bravely preparing for the worst. He had suffered no other symptoms, but he put that down to the aggressive preventative action he had taken, having consumed vast quantities of aspirin, ibuprofen, cough medicines and nasal sprays, and a few indigestion remedies as well, just for safety.

This had left the Scarecrow partnerless, and although the epidemic had ensured that quite a few others would be looking for partners, whomever he asked seemed to have just managed to find someone. Then again, there were some people whom the Scarecrow was too scared to play with. On this list were Dorothy's Auntie Em and Uncle Henry. Having been reassured that they were both in good health and definitely playing together, he phoned their farm to see if one of the farmhands would be interested in playing with him. Auntie Em answered.

"No, Zeke and Hickory can't come out to play," she told him. She believed that all people younger than she was should be treated as children, while all those older were at least halfway to losing their marbles. The Scarecrow was about to ring off when she added, "But we have a new lad here, name of Hank. I'll send him along."

The Scarecrow had a feeling that he had heard of him. Yes, this must be Hank the Hunk — not so named for his appearance but because of the suspicion that his brain was made of solid wood.

"Isn't he the one who has been in the beginners' class for five years?"

"Yep," said Auntie Em. "Not annoyed because he broke your record, I hope?"

"But from what I've heard, he really hasn't got a clue!" the Scarecrow responded.

"That's why it's so important that more experienced players..." she coughed involuntarily, "...partner him occasionally to allow him to see how he can develop," Em responded, almost choking with the unaccustomed effort of being tactful.

And so was born a partnership like no other in the Club, or probably anywhere else in the civilized world — or beyond, for that matter.

The Club had recently purchased a set of Bridgemates for scoring, and, as he and Hank were North-South and sitting throughout, the Scarecrow had taken charge of the machine. This was a good safety play. Hank needed most of his concentration simply to hold all thirteen cards. The remainder was required to follow suit. He had not yet been known to manage to muster enough concentration to hope to play the cards in the right order.

The Scarecrow had the advantage over Hank in that he never really bothered much about concentration. He knew that no matter how much he tried, it rarely improved his results. Indeed, the Tin Man had told him that the best part of his game, apart from shuffling and dealing (and these were becoming redundant with the introduction of new technology), was that he played the cards rapidly in whatever order they appeared. Better to leave matters of good card play to Lady Luck, rather than take too active an interest in this part of the game himself.

Their first opponents that evening were the unusual partnership of the Wicked Witch of the West, sitting West, of course, and the Irritable Witch of the South, sitting East and distinctly grumpy about it. Glinda, the Wicked Witch's usual partner, was missing, supposedly one of the flu victims. There had been speculation, however, that the illness might have less to do with the virus than the curses she had been subjected to the previous week when she went down in a small slam with twelve top tricks.

"It's good to see you getting practice in taking finesses, Glinda," her partner had begun, before the thin veil of politeness dropped. There was less speculation about the missing Unpleasant Witch of the North. She had taken great delight in coughing and spluttering over everyone the previous week and was no doubt deeply disappointed by the number of her opponents who were still fit to play.

This was the first hand of the evening:

♠ 2
♡ A 6 4
♢ Q 7 3
♣ A K Q J 3 2
_____
♠ Q 9 6 4
♡ Q 10 7 5
♢ K J 4 2
♣ 7

The auction was not a thing of beauty. With no one vulnerable, it went:

West	North	East	South
Wicked	*Hank*	*Irritable*	*Scarecrow*
	1♣	pass	1♡
pass	2♣	pass	2♢
pass	3♣	pass	3NT
all pass			

West led the ♠3.

The Scarecrow focused on the Bridgemate as the young farmhand laid down the dummy. Feeling nervous playing with a partner as accomplished as the Scarecrow (after all, the Scarecrow played regularly on a team with the Tin Man and Dorothy), Hank felt he had to explain himself.

"I was very worried about the spade suit, so I thought it best to try to play in clubs. I still think Five Clubs might be better; what do you think?"

The Scarecrow was too focused on trying to enter the contract into the machine.

"What do I do now? Oh yes, I press 'OK.' Yes, Five Clubs would probably be a reasonable bid; after all, you've no losers in the suit."

He entered Five Clubs by South in the Bridgemate.

The Scarecrow looked at the dummy cursorily and called for dummy's singleton to be played. It didn't cross his mind to wonder if partner should have given heart preference with three-card support. After all, many of his partners were reluctant to do so with four. East, the Irritable Witch, won the first trick with the ♠A and returned the ♠J to the queen and her partner's king. The Scarecrow played the ♣2 from dummy and called for the ace.

"It's customary," said the Irritable Witch in her crustiest tone, "for the winner of the previous trick to lead to the next one. Perhaps we should honor that custom."

"But I ruffed that trick," squeaked the Scarecrow, horribly aware that he was about to experience another of the many awful things that seemed to happen to him.

"An original tactic in Three Notrump," commented the Wicked Witch.

"But, but, but…" twittered the Scarecrow as he realized his error, "I wouldn't have played a club had I known."

"That's a shame," said the Irritable Witch, winning her partner's spade return with the ten, the Scarecrow randomly throwing dummy's ◊3. The Irritable Witch now cashed the ◊A and led her last spade to the Scarecrow's nine, with her partner, the Wicked Witch, following low. After a brief pause, the Irritable Witch rounded on the Scarecrow.

"Will dummy be joining us in this trick?" she asked bitterly. "This really is becoming impossible."

The Scarecrow, now in a complete tizzy, reached over and threw the ♡4, following it up with the ♡5 from hand.

"Oh no, I didn't meant to play that. You see, I had just played a heart and I thought — "

"Is it possible for you to concentrate for one second?" snapped the Irritable Witch. "And that card is played." She jabbed at the ♡5.

Meanwhile, something very unusual had happened — the Wicked Witch of the West had gone silent. Where there was stirring to do and a good chance of upsetting the opponents, she was usually to the fore. However, she had started with:

♠ K 7 5 3   ♡ K J 2   ◊ 10   ♣ 10 9 8 6 5

And the position now was:

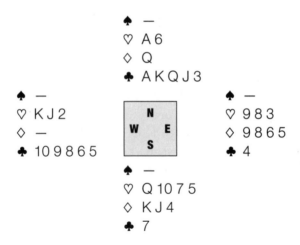

```
              ♠ —
              ♡ A 6
              ◇ Q
              ♣ A K Q J 3
♠ —                          ♠ —
♡ K J 2      ┌─────────┐     ♡ 9 8 3
◇ —          │    N    │     ◇ 9 8 6 5
♣ 10 9 8 6 5 │  W   E  │     ♣ 4
             │    S    │
             └─────────┘
              ♠ —
              ♡ Q 10 7 5
              ◇ K J 4
              ♣ 7
```

Forced to lead the heart from hand, the Scarecrow won in dummy with the ace, as the Wicked Witch, with a strong sense of foreboding, played low. With four tricks in the bag, she had felt quite confident that the Scarecrow would just run his club suit and find the bad news of the 5-1 split too late. But now...

The Scarecrow played dummy's ◇Q and overtook it with his ◇K, then cashed the ◇J, throwing the small heart from dummy. He was about to claim five club tricks when he noticed that West had discarded the ♡J and the ♡K on the diamond winners. It always astonished him how players rated so much better than he was managed to make such trivial errors. Cashing the ♡Q, he claimed his nine tricks.

Three minutes later, after the Scarecrow had worked out how to enter the result into the Bridgemate, the Irritable Witch reluctantly pressed the OK button, acknowledging a score of 400 for North-South. No one noticed that it actually showed Five Clubs making, a score that would later cause much discussion as all wondered how this contract could possibly have come home. Despite lengthy questioning in the bar, the Scarecrow and Hank were unable to recount the sequence of plays to people who sought an explanation as to how this hapless pair had managed third place. The two men were oblivious to the looks of amazement and simply thrilled with their result.

The winter flu virus continued to plague the Club over the coming days, and so it was that the formidable partnership of the Scarecrow and Hank had a second outing the following week.

Since that first game, the bar had reverberated with tales of what they had done to their opponents. Having started with the two witches, they had continued to have an uncanny knack of landing on their feet. Their good scores certainly had nothing to do with skill. Rumors abounded that a fairy godmother was looking after them, although Auntie Em had been heard to mutter something about the devil looking after his own. Their results did have one very positive feature appreciated by all — no one was short of a hard-luck story, which is, after all, the staple diet of bridge players worldwide.

Hank was more nervous than ever this second time out. Auntie Em had told him originally that any score over 30 percent would be a triumph, and the pressure of having to continue such a good performance was weighing heavily on him. To add to his problems, he had really struggled with using the bidding box and wasn't looking forward to having to do it again. He had enough problems coping with the thirteen cards in his hand; he now also had to look after two sets of bidding cards: 35 bids in one socket containing everything from One Club to Seven Notrump, and lots of passes, doubles, redoubles, stop cards, and alert cards in the other socket. It had taken half of the committee four days to reassemble the contents of his box from the week before, with the cards being found in a variety of unlikely locations. Indeed, the Five Spade ticket did not reappear until it was found in a trifle at the Christmas party.

Hank's worst fear came to pass when he found that this time they would be moving. He was sitting West, and they'd be changing tables after every three boards: he had received a lot of criticism for destroying one bidding box and was worried about how much carnage he might cause during a circuit of the room. By the time he left each table, his bidding box had lost any semblance of a neat and tidy appearance, much to the annoyance of the Honorary Chairman of the Lollipop Guild, who was following him. As they started the last of the

three boards against the Irritable Witch of the South and the now recovered Unpleasant Witch of the North, One Club to Three Clubs were in the front compartment, green passes, red doubles and blue redoubles were thoroughly shuffled, and the stop and alert cards were probably somewhere within twenty feet of the table.

The Irritable Witch of the South was dealer and held the following hand:

♠AQ82 ♡A874 ◇KJ8 ♣KQ

The two witches liked changing their systems regularly, putting in anything that might rile their opponents and then moving on to something else when they found the other Club members getting used to it. The primary purpose of any convention for this pair was to upset and annoy the opposition. Once it failed to do that, it had outlived its usefulness.

Their latest ideas were based on an aggressive set of two-level openers. Foremost among them was the Irritable Witch's favorite toy: Two Diamonds showed either a 19-20 balanced hand or a weak hand with both majors. With her balanced

19-count, she had a perfect opportunity to use it. Opponents had a habit of coming into the auction expecting the weak variety, and she relished the thought of another opportunity to take a big penalty, with the inevitable consequential arguments between East and West. She and her partner would then take great delight in entering the fray and adding fuel to the flames.

Disappointingly, Hank, on her left, passed over Two Diamonds. Her partner bid Two Spades, showing where she would prefer to play if opener held the weak version. Her Two Notrump now cleared matters up, and over the Three Club ask, her Three Diamonds showed she had at least one four-card major.

This was all very boring for Hank, sitting over her in the West seat. He had had a run of good cards and was now looking at a 6-count. His mind wandered. He grabbed his coffee with his left hand, and then pulled the pass card with his right hand, so it wasn't until the auction was over that he found his third pass was undeniably red.

The Unpleasant Witch of the North now bid Three Hearts, which told her partner that she had a four-card spade suit. The Scarecrow, sitting East, didn't really understand systems. He certainly had no idea what was going on, and it seemed to him to be insubordination to ask his betters what their bids meant. After all, he didn't usually know what his own meant, and if he didn't ask others, they might not ask him embarrassing questions during the auction.

What he did know was that partner had doubled Three Diamonds, and he had a five-card heart suit over this Three Heart bid. Doubling seemed the right thing to do.

The Irritable Witch of the South now realized with annoyance that her toy had wrong-sided the potential Four Spade contract, due to her partner's Two Spade response. It was wrong-sided in two ways. First, a diamond lead would come through her honors with every chance that Hank would be able to give the Scarecrow a ruff on the third round. Second, and more importantly, she would be in the unfortunate situation of being dummy. She and her partner did not agree on many things, but they both held very similar views on declarer play: each knew herself to be far better at it than her partner, and each resented the indignity of having to watch her partner butcher the play. The situation called for imaginative bidding, so disdaining the known 4-4 spade fit, the Irritable Witch bid Three Notrump.

The remainder of the auction was routine. Hank had been startled into a higher level of consciousness by his partner's red card. He was very far from sure of what was happening, but assumed that he had to do something over the Scarecrow's double. He doubled with a feeling that this might be what was meant by following partner's defense. South's redouble was even more routine. Her opposition's known ability in defense was worth at least two tricks, and, anyway, the redouble would certainly rattle them.

The full auction had been:

West	North	East	South
Hank	Unpleasant	Scarecrow	Irritable
			2◇*
pass	2♠*	pass	2NT
pass	3♣*	pass	3◇*
dbl	3♡*	dbl	3NT
dbl	pass	pass	redbl
all pass			

The Scarecrow had loaned Hank several erudite books on initial leads. He hadn't understood any of them, but, if asked, could give the names of Mike Lawrence or Andrew Robson or Kelsey Matheson. He was sure these people knew what they were doing, and it sounded good to say that he followed their advice. On this occasion, he remembered his partner's double of Three Hearts, and just in case that showed hearts, he decided to lead one, the five. Dummy was spread:

```
          ♠ K 9 4 3
          ♡ K 10
          ◇ 10 2
          ♣ J 8 7 6 4
          ┌─────────┐
          └─────────┘
          ♠ A Q 8 2
          ♡ A 8 7 4
          ◇ K J 8
          ♣ K Q
```

The hand was an open book to a competent player like the Irritable Witch of the South. She won the lead in dummy and led a club, taken by West's ace. Hank continued with his partner's suit, leading the ♡2.

The Irritable Witch took this, cashed the ♣Q and played three rounds of spades, ending in dummy after the Scarecrow, East, showed up with three in that suit, and Hank, West, discarded a diamond. She now played the ♣J, the Scarecrow discarding a diamond, and as she led the penultimate club from dummy, she sat back in quiet contentment. Hank was out of spades and hearts, so on winning the fourth club, he would have to play diamonds around to her. The Irritable Witch wondered if he would cash the ◇A and then play into her king-jack, or play a small one. Either way, she would have ten tricks. A small diamond appeared, and she laid down her remaining cards with a flourish.

"I'll win this, then take a spade and the last club for plus one, thank you very much," she said.

The Scarecrow looked distinctly uncomfortable as he played the ◇A. He was sure the Irritable Witch knew what she was talking about, but he really thought that his three remaining cards, all hearts, were winners.

The full hand was:

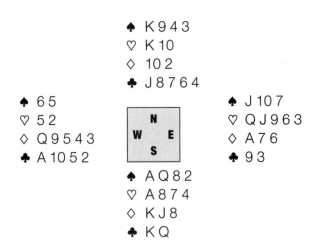

```
                    ♠ K 9 4 3
                    ♡ K 10
                    ◊ 10 2
                    ♣ J 8 7 6 4
♠ 6 5                               ♠ J 10 7
♡ 5 2              N                ♡ Q J 9 6 3
◊ Q 9 5 4 3    W       E            ◊ A 7 6
♣ A 10 5 2         S                ♣ 9 3
                    ♠ A Q 8 2
                    ♡ A 8 7 4
                    ◊ K J 8
                    ♣ K Q
```

The Irritable Witch spluttered with rage as she picked up Hank's hand. "How can you double Three Diamonds with that load of rubbish?"

"Well done, partner," started the Unpleasant Witch of the North. "I suppose you've never seen either of our two opponents in action before. Is that why you chose to believe their bidding, or was it just crass stupidity? The contract could be made by any Munchkin on that lead, although a Munchkin might have opted for the more normal contract of Four Spades, which I couldn't fail to make.

"In Three Notrump, play three rounds of spades immediately, and then if that fool in the West seat discards a club, you can set up four tricks in clubs with your nine of spades as an entry. If he discards a diamond, you can now safely get one diamond trick and two club tricks. If he discards a heart, he can't do you any harm when he wins his ace of clubs."

The Unpleasant Witch of the North was in her element. She had no qualms about using double dummy analysis to criticize her partner. It was worth getting a bad score to have her partner squirming this much!

6

Some Like It Hot

January dragged on to its end, as only January can. With it went the flu epidemic that had been sweeping through the Over the Rainbow Bridge Club. As the days slowly lengthened, the number of tables in play returned to normal, and the regular partnerships reappeared. Normal hostilities were resumed.

The winter weather presented new opportunities for malevolence from the Wicked Witch of the West and her coven, which they seized with delight. Outside, the temperatures remained low as February progressed. Inside, it was a more complicated picture.

During the first tournament of the month, players were woken up early in the session by the cry of the Irritable Witch of the South: "It's freezing in here! Someone turn up the heat!"

The tournament director, a well-meaning Munchkin, came over to the table. "Oh dear, I'm sorry about that," she said. "It feels okay to me, but we could turn it up a little."

"What?" squawked the Unpleasant Witch of the North. "I'm boiling alive over here. If you make it any hotter I think I shall faint, and I shall hold you responsible!"

The tournament director scratched her head. How could there be any temperature difference between these two particular seats? She was at a loss as to what to do. For the rest of the night, various small changes were tried in order to satisfy the conflicting needs of the North and South witches. The table was moved. Doors were opened, closed, or left ajar. The windows were brought into play. Nothing seemed to work. The tournament director left the club that night in a state of exhaustion.

The whole question of the ambient temperature was a source of delight to the witches. It opened up countless opportunities for creating aggravation and unpleasantness in the Club. Just last year, the committee, in a desperate attempt to resolve matters, had put in a full air-conditioning system at great expense. The Wicked Witch of the West had taken charge of the project, which had proved quite disruptive for several weeks. She had worked tirelessly to ensure that it was completed on time; the opportunity to terrify the workmen into obedience was all the reward she asked for. This was the first winter with the new system and all the members of the committee were desperately hoping it would bring an end to this source of intermember conflict. It was a triumph of hope over experience. They should have known better. Though the situation seemed to have improved, this was to prove a dawn of the false variety: the witches would not let go of such an easy source of pleasure.

The second tournament of the month was worse. For no readily apparent reason, the witches of the North and South switched to East-West, an almost unprecedented occurrence. Even more bizarrely, as they marauded around the room, they seemed to bring the weather with them. Dorothy and the Tin Man had been sitting quite comfortably all evening observing the chaos.

"Mass hysteria, hallucinations," the Tin Man said, snorting. "They make such a fuss that they convince their opponents they can feel it too. Slightest breath of air and people are going crazy."

Late in the tournament, the witches swept across to their table. Settling quickly, they all drew their cards for the first board.

Dealer South. Neither vul.

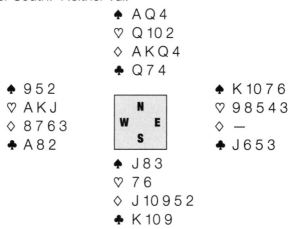

```
                    ♠ A Q 4
                    ♡ Q 10 2
                    ◊ A K Q 4
                    ♣ Q 7 4
  ♠ 9 5 2                           ♠ K 10 7 6
  ♡ A K J          N                ♡ 9 8 5 4 3
  ◊ 8 7 6 3     W      E            ◊ —
  ♣ A 8 2          S                ♣ J 6 5 3
                    ♠ J 8 3
                    ♡ 7 6
                    ◊ J 10 9 5 2
                    ♣ K 10 9
```

Playing their usual five-card majors and strong notrump, the Irritable Witch opened One Diamond in second seat. The Tin Man, sitting North, was too strong for One Notrump and doubled. East, the Unpleasant Witch, passed. Dorothy decided to stretch a little and bid One Notrump since none of her suits were appealing. The Tin Man ended the auction with a jump to Three Notrump.

West	North	East	South
Irritable	*Tin Man*	*Unpleasant*	*Dorothy*
			pass
1◊	dbl	pass	1NT
pass	3NT	all pass	

The Irritable Witch led the ♡A. The Tin Man tabled dummy, commenting on the quality of declarer's diamond stopper. As Dorothy considered the hand, the Unpleasant Witch pulled a handkerchief out of her handbag and started mopping her brow.

"Absolutely stifling in this corner," she moaned to Dorothy. "How could you put up with this all night? I suppose him being cold-blooded, he won't have noticed." For the first time, it occurred to Dorothy that she did feel rather hot.

Winning the first trick, the Irritable Witch followed up with the ♡K and then the ♡J. It looked from the carding as if hearts were 5-3. Dorothy had five diamond tricks, the ♠A, and a heart on top. She could establish a club trick, and the positions of the ♠K and the ♣J would determine her chances. She decided to drive out the ♣A. She led up to the king, losing to the ace.

The Irritable Witch promptly put the ♠2 on the table — it might persuade Dorothy she had the king, and she didn't care if she deceived her partner. Indeed, she rather enjoyed doing so!

Dorothy now felt sure about the heart split. She tried to recap the play so far.

"So airless," the Unpleasant Witch muttered loudly. "Hard to think with so little oxygen."

Yes, Dorothy could feel her concentration going. West had definitely shown 12 points, and clearly had a balanced hand, having opened what was at most a four-card suit. If she had the ♠K, she would have opened One Notrump, so there was no point in taking the finesse, which was certain to lose. Dorothy won the ace and played off her diamonds.

The Unpleasant Witch had a lot of discards to make from the East hand. She had thrown a club and a spade easily enough, and on the third round she had bared her ♠K. On the fourth, she pitched a heart. With four cards left, this was the position:

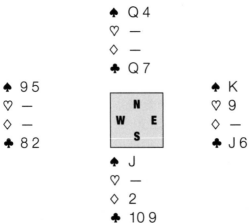

```
              ♠ Q 4
              ♡ —
              ◊ —
              ♣ Q 7
  ♠ 9 5                      ♠ K
  ♡ —          N             ♡ 9
  ◊ —       W     E          ◊ —
  ♣ 8 2        S             ♣ J 6
              ♠ J
              ♡ —
              ◊ 2
              ♣ 10 9
```

Dorothy played her last diamond, West and dummy throwing spades. With no winning option, the Unpleasant Witch threw her last heart winner, hoping Dorothy would take the club finesse. However, the position of the jack was irrelevant to her. With the hand an open book, Dorothy put the Unpleasant Witch on lead with the ♠K, forcing her to play a club to concede the ninth trick.

The Tin Man was shifting uncomfortably in his seat. Determined not to acknowledge the unaccountably warm atmosphere, but starting to feel tetchy, he commented, "Interesting. It was kind of West to tell you the complete lie of the cards."

This was the second board of the set.

Dealer West. N/S vul.

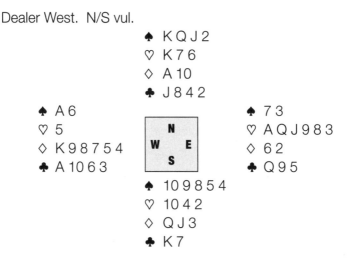

As dealer, the Irritable Witch was taking some time to sort her cards, delaying the start of the auction.

"So cold!" she hissed. "Feels like the cards have frozen together." Dorothy glanced over at her. She was about to comment on Irritable's unusual earrings but stopped herself. They looked like — no, they couldn't really be icicles, could they?

Once again, the Irritable Witch opened One Diamond. This time, the Tin Man was slightly too light for One Notrump, but in any case, he had a decent shape for a takeout double. After One Heart by the Unpleasant Witch, Dorothy bid One Spade. Always pleased not to have to raise her partner, the Irritable

Witch showed her second suit with a bid of Two Clubs. The Tin Man's raise to Two Spades was followed by a slow pass from East and quicker ones by South and West.

West	North	East	South
Irritable	*Tin Man*	*Unpleasant*	*Dorothy*
1◇	dbl	1♡	1♠
2♣	2♠	all pass	

The Irritable Witch led her heart, and East's jack won. The Unpleasant Witch pondered her next move. If her partner's heart was a singleton, then there was no rush to continue the suit. Ace and another would merely swap her sure heart trick for one of her partner's trumps. If the Irritable Witch and Dorothy both had doubletons, then playing ace and another might promote a trump trick, but that seemed very unlikely. A trump didn't look as if it would achieve much. A club looked dangerous with the jack in the dummy. A diamond? Yes, if the Irritable Witch held the king and jack, then a diamond through could set up a trick for her. Indeed, a diamond switch might be necessary to prevent Irritable from being endplayed at a later point and forced to lead away from the king. Feeling ready for any post-mortem argument, she switched to the ◇6.

Dorothy breathed a mental sigh of relief. Come to think of it, she could actually see her breath! She had dodged a bullet. After three rounds of hearts, the defense would still have had both black aces to take. To have the values for her opening bid, the Irritable Witch must have the ♣A. It was clear to Dorothy she would have needed a miracle to avoid a second loser in the suit.

The diamond switch ran around to the ten. The ♠K drove out the ace and the Irritable Witch played a second diamond. The ♠Q drew the outstanding trumps. Dorothy could see some light emerging at the end of the tunnel. West's failure to continue hearts made it certain that they were splitting 6-1. In that case, she might be able to develop a second club trick and discard one of her losing hearts. The first step was to lead a club to the king. West won the ace and played the ◇K, ruffed in the dummy. The Unpleasant Witch threw a heart. Dorothy had won four of the first seven tricks. She had three trumps to come and needed to find one more winner. This was the position:

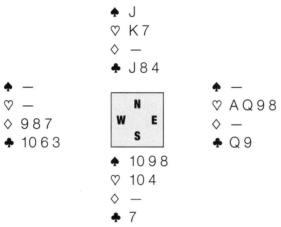

```
              ♠ J
              ♡ K 7
              ◇ —
              ♣ J 8 4
♠ —                        ♠ —
♡ —          N            ♡ A Q 9 8
◇ 9 8 7    W   E          ◇ —
♣ 10 6 3      S            ♣ Q 9
              ♠ 10 9 8
              ♡ 10 4
              ◇ —
              ♣ 7
```

Dorothy felt an icy gust of air around her legs. Feeling suddenly stiff, the Tin Man groaned and stretched his right leg.

"Forgot your WD-40?" the Irritable Witch cackled.

This is ridiculous, thought Dorothy. How can I be getting frostbite on the left side of my face and sunburn on the right? She led a small club from the dummy. By playing the nine, the Unpleasant Witch avoided immediately setting up another trick for declarer. She could see that leaving her partner on lead was hopeless: she would either have to set up a club or a heart trick in the dummy. Overtaking with the ten, the Irritable Witch then realized that she was in no better a position. A diamond would give a ruff and discard. She tried another club. Dorothy shrugged and called for the jack — with the nine and ten gone, either it would score or she would ruff the queen and the eight would be the master.

"Lucky club position," snarled the Irritable Witch.

"Well, I was going to be on a guess at worst. If your partner had two of the three clubs outstanding above the eight, then I couldn't go wrong. If she had none of them, then I couldn't go wrong. If she had only one of them it would have come down to guessing whether to play the jack or eight on the third round of the suit," Dorothy replied. "So I was always going to have some play for it."

"At least you were after Trick 2," cut in the Tin Man, speaking hurriedly. "Strange pair of boards. You made the first hand because you had the ten and nine of clubs and the second because you held the eight and seven. We will need to think about amending our methods to take these key cards into account."

"And we'll have to amend ours, too," screeched the Irritable Witch. "The cold seems to have made my partner's minute brain seize up."

The Unpleasant Witch was working on a suitably caustic riposte when the Tin Man jumped to his feet and strode off, flexing his leg painfully. As he elbowed his way through the crowd of players haranguing the Club president, the Honorary Chairman of the Lollipop Guild, his voice could be heard clearly from across the room.

"The committee has to do something about this! The atmospheric conditions are unbearable!"

The Chairman promised to address the matter with the greatest urgency. The angry crowd of players only let him leave the club once he had phoned all the other committee members, informing them of an emergency meeting to take place the following day.

 Exodus

Auntie Em was exhausted! The committee meeting had finished at four thirty in the morning. If they had been discussing bridge, she might have enjoyed it. She would have preferred even the normal topics of committee meetings, such as the latest ideas from the witches on how to infringe the rules without quite breaking them, or another case of the Tin Man upsetting some Munchkins. She was even looking back nostalgically on committee meetings of thirty years past, when all that was ever discussed were the latest ideas on rules about smoking.

This time, the only issue on the agenda had been the new air conditioning system. It was causing chaos. It would have been simple had there been a single issue of it being too hot, or too cold, or too stuffy, or too drafty! But there wasn't! Everyone seemed to have a different view of what the problem was, and worse still, it changed depending on not just where you were sitting, but when! The Wicked Witch of the West held court throughout the discussion and clearly enjoyed being the expert authority on the topic. For every complaint, she had a deep, technical explanation. By eleven o'clock, the other members of the committee were exhausted; by midnight, they each felt as if their brain had been rubbed with a Brillo pad; by two o'clock, they would have agreed to anything; and by four o'clock, several were suicidal. But the Wicked Witch persisted.

Finally, she proposed that a full review was essential and that in the meantime, the Over the Rainbow Bridge Club should temporarily abandon its premises. This was agreed unanimously; the rest of the committee would have agreed to anything just to get home!

The next day, the club president found them short-term accommodation at a local hotel. It had an upstairs function room that was just the right size. That same evening, the club held its first session there, and it didn't take long for difficulties to emerge. To the surprise of no one, it was one of the witches who seemed to have the major problem with the new facility.

The Unpleasant Witch of the North had a bad hip. Bravely, she had not complained about this before, but with the bar and the toilet downstairs, each of her many trips to one or the other took an excruciating time to complete. This problem was at its worst on their third night in the new premises. It was the annual Individual tournament and without a partner to anchor her, the Unpleasant Witch was regularly making her way to the wrong table on her reentry to the room.

During an early enforced break while the tournament director tried to sort out another witch-inspired glitch in the movement, the Tin Man collared the club president, the Honorary Chairman of the Lollipop Guild.

"When do we move back? Why hasn't the air conditioning been sorted yet?" he snapped by way of an opening pleasantry.

"I must say, I must say, it is a most extraordinary situation," the Chairman replied. "It seems that the only member of the committee who knows how the system works is the Wicked Witch of the West. As you know, she has been away since the committee meeting. She should be back next week."

"What about the company that installed it?"

The Chairman leaned in confidentially. "You will recall that the Wicked Witch oversaw the installation... It seems that our club has been blacklisted by the company, I'm afraid. We have managed to find an independent engineer. He is actually at the club as we speak. I am hoping to be able to make an announcement at the end of play. I think we all recognize that the current arrangement is not satisfactory. Can you imagine holding the annual general meeting here?" He shuddered.

"But that's still six weeks away! Surely the problems will have been resolved long before then?" The Tin Man looked visibly shaken.

The bridge did not improve his mood. At the end of the session, he and Dorothy made their way from the card room to the bar in search of solace.

"Remind me never, ever, ever to enter this tournament again," groaned the Tin Man as they stood on the stairs in the line that had formed behind the Unpleasant Witch of the North.

"I did," replied Dorothy. "As I did last year, and the year before. You should know by now what the club Individual is like. How did you score?"

"I personally played a 70 percent game. My idiot partners played a 30 percent game with me, then became inspired when playing against me. In fact, they may have been playing against me the whole time."

Finally, they got to the bar.

"Tell me a good horror story," said Dorothy. The Tin Man tried to piece together the fragments of his scorecard while she ordered the drinks. "Tell me about the one that made you take up origami."

"Origami is paper folding, not tear — " he began to say, but before he could complete his pedantry, the Lion and the Scarecrow joined them.

"I got a good score on Board 7," the Lion said, preening himself. "Listen to this."

Dealer South. Both vul.

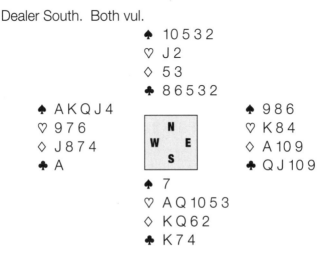

♠ 10 5 3 2
♡ J 2
◊ 5 3
♣ 8 6 5 3 2

♠ A K Q J 4
♡ 9 7 6
◊ J 8 7 4
♣ A

♠ 9 8 6
♡ K 8 4
◊ A 10 9
♣ Q J 10 9

♠ 7
♡ A Q 10 5 3
◊ K Q 6 2
♣ K 7 4

"I was South. I opened One Heart. West overcalled One Spade. Despite his wasted king of hearts, East showed a sound raise to Three Spades with a cuebid, and West, despite his rotten hearts and diamonds, jumped to Four Spades. You know me — controlled aggression — but this was just macho overbidding! Anyway, partner led the jack of hearts and continued when declarer ducked in dummy. After taking my three heart tricks, I switched to the king of diamonds. No way was he going to make after that! That was my first board. Do you guys know how the sheet turned out?"

"What a defense!" said the Tin Man. "Just look at the hand. If you don't switch to diamonds, declarer must lose two tricks in the suit."

"Yeah, well, a plus score is a plus score," growled the Lion defensively.

The Tin Man turned to the Scarecrow. "I'm sure you would like to tell everyone about your performance on this hand. Tell the Lion how you managed to out-defend him by two tricks," he said as he slumped back in his chair.

The Scarecrow, who had gone red, began his tale: "You see, it was really the fault of that ghastly Irritable Witch of the South" he said apologetically. "She was so unpleasant when we sat opposite each other. She said 'Don't revoke, don't lead out of turn, count your cards, lead back my suit, and bid one less if you think you might play the hand.' I mean, I know I do lose attention sometimes, but there is no need to speak like that." Dorothy muttered agreement, the Tin Man was silent, and the Lion had a sudden coughing fit.

"Anyway, we had a similar start to the auction, except that East raised to Two Spades, which I think was a very good bid!" He glanced at the Tin Man. "I doubled and West competed to Three Spades. The Irritable Witch of the South led the jack of hearts, and, like the Lion, I won the first three tricks. I thought I would teach her a lesson. 'Lead back my suit' she had said, so I thought that was just what I would do. I played another heart, even though I knew it was giving a ruff and dis-card — honestly I did." He looked appealingly to the Tin Man, who just snorted.

The Scarecrow continued: "Looking at all the hands, I can see that declarer would have been in a lot of trouble if he had ruffed. I suppose he knew I would be short in trumps because I had doubled Two Spades. Anyway, he threw away a diamond. The Irritable Witch ruffed with the ten of spades, so he threw a diamond from the dummy too. Partner played a diamond. Declarer won the ace and drew trumps but in the end I got the king and queen of diamonds. That meant he was two down in Three Spades."

"Too much to ask that declarer would try to ruff a diamond in the dummy, of course," said the Tin Man, scowling. "Dia-bolical, illogical play all round!"

"I don't see why you are so upset about it," said Dorothy. "What did you do on the hand?"

"Me? Very little, other than sit with a harpy on my right, an idiot in front of me, and the Scarecrow on my left! The hand is a death trap. The inspired defense found by our friend leaves declarer lying with his throat cut even in Three Spades. I'm afraid your +100 is nothing special, Lion." The Tin Man felt some comfort in finding company in misfortune.

"Well, actually," said Dorothy, "I made Three Spades on the ruff and discard defense the Scarecrow found." The others looked at her incredulously. "On the fourth heart, a trump, high or low, is no good, and we have seen how horrible it gets if you throw a diamond. The only thing left was to discard my ace of clubs. North ruffed high and played a diamond. I won the ace and took the ruffing finesse in clubs. After I had ruffed out the king of clubs, I was able to draw trumps in three rounds, ending in the dummy with the nine now an entry. The clubs allowed me to discard all my losing diamonds."

The Tin Man nodded and raised his glass mechanically. After a moment's reflection, he scribbled down another hand. "How did we all do on this one? Three Notrump by East, I would expect?"

Dealer East. N/S vul.

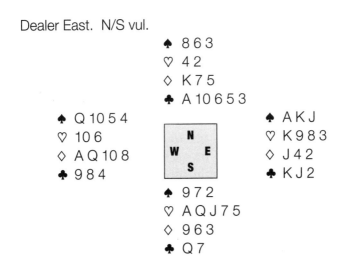

♠ 863
♡ 42
◇ K 7 5
♣ A 10 6 5 3

♠ Q 10 5 4   ♠ A K J
♡ 10 6   ♡ K 9 8 3
◇ A Q 10 8   ◇ J 4 2
♣ 9 8 4   ♣ K J 2

♠ 9 7 2
♡ A Q J 7 5
◇ 9 6 3
♣ Q 7

"Sorry, I don't remember it," said the Scarecrow.

"I do," said Dorothy. "Yes, I played Three Notrump from the East seat. I had shown hearts over Stayman, which put South off leading them. She led a diamond, which I lost to North's king. He played back a low club. I can't see any reason to get it right. I put in the jack. South won the queen and played back a second club. North won and played a heart through. They had five tricks before I had drawn breath. I wondered if I could have made it if I had gone up with the king of clubs, run the pointed suits, and sort of strip-squeezed South?" Dorothy ticked off the cards.

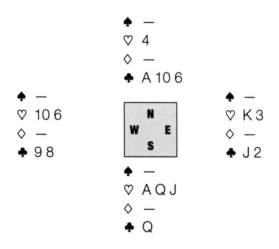

"I would have had eight tricks at this point and if I ducked a club, South would have been endplayed into giving me my ninth in hearts."

"Nice try, but not good enough," said the Tin Man. "North can defeat you by going up with the ace of clubs and playing a heart through. And keeping an extra heart would do you no good, because that would mean baring the jack of clubs, at which point North's clubs would run. Anyway, we are well into the realms of the double dummy. No one would play this hand like that. This hand, however, is a different matter." He wrote out an amended hand and slapped it in front of the Scarecrow. "Recognize it now?" he asked.

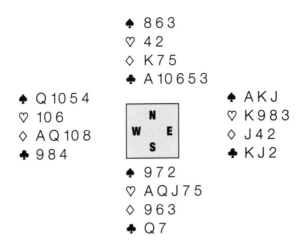

```
                    ♠ 8 6 3
                    ♡ 4 2
                    ◇ K 7 5
                    ♣ A 10 6 5 3
  ♠ Q 10 5 4                        ♠ A K J
  ♡ 10 6          ┌─────────┐      ♡ K 9 8 3
  ◇ A Q 10 8      │   N     │      ◇ J 4 2
  ♣ 9 8 4         │ W     E │      ♣ K J 2
                  │   S     │
                  └─────────┘
                    ♠ 9 7 2
                    ♡ A Q J 7 5
                    ◇ 9 6 3
                    ♣ Q 7
```

"I was North. Our charming, or should I say charmed, friend held the East cards. The auction was as at Dorothy's table. By the way, why didn't you convert Three Notrump to Four Spades?" The Scarecrow opened his mouth but no sound came out.

"Never mind," the Tin Man continued. "Despite himself he had reached the normal contract. My partner also led a diamond. I also won the king and returned a small club. Now, to be fair, there is no reason at all to choose the king or the jack. It is a guess, which for the Scarecrow is the same as a certainty. He won the king. Would you care to take over, maestro?"

"Well..." The Scarecrow marshalled his thoughts. "I could see four spade tricks, three diamond tricks, one club trick, and the best chance for a ninth seemed to be to lead up to the king of hearts. I wanted to put that off for as long as possible because I was a bit worried about clubs." The Tin Man snorted.

The Scarecrow ignored him and continued, "I thought I would cash my winners, trying to finish in the dummy before trying the heart. At least that way I would have eight tricks." He looked around for support. Dorothy and the Lion nodded, trying to look more encouraging than bemused.

"So, anyway, I took the diamonds. South threw a spade, then the ace and king of spades. I decided to cross over to dummy to take the last two. I played my small spade and then realized I had had a hand sorting problem, again." He blushed.

"Allow me to retake the reins," jumped in the Tin Man with masochistic relish. "Look at the position we had stumbled into:

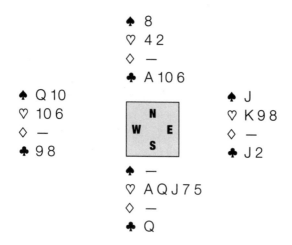

It is similar to the one Dorothy sketched out a minute ago except that everyone has two more cards. Yet now the strip squeeze has worked! By playing his non-pointy, though undoubtedly black, two of clubs, declarer gave the defense an insoluble problem. If South is left on lead, the defense must concede a heart trick. If North overtakes then the jack of clubs is established and the defense can take no more than two heart tricks before declarer regains the lead. If he doesn't, South is endplayed. Sheer genius."

He finished his drink and looked around. "Same again everyone? Now Dorothy, as I was saying, never, ever, ever..."

He was interrupted by the Honorary Chairman of the Lollipop Guild's call for attention. "Fellow members! Fellow members! Your attention, please. The heating engineer has returned from our club. I'm sure you will all want to hear what he has to say!"

A young man stood before them wearing a startled look, clearly not having expected to be reporting back to such an audience. Various people shouted out.

"So, what have you found?"

"Is it fixed?"

"When can we go back?"

The Chairman hushed everyone, then addressed the engineer. "Well, well. You can see how keen our members are to hear your findings. What can you tell us all? Why is our system malfunctioning, and what can be done about it?"

The engineer shifted uncomfortably from one foot to the other. "To be honest, I have never seen anything like it."

"But can you fix it?"

"The thing is, it isn't broken. It is working perfectly. It has to be the most sophisticated setup I have ever seen. The way it has been broken into zones, the different settings, the range of timings across the zones... it's all extraordinary. Whoever set it up is a genius!"

There were dark mutterings round the room. The words "witch," "west," and "wicked" echoed in whispers. The Chairman remained statesmanlike and hushed the crowd.

"I presume that setting can be undone. Can you return it to its original settings?"

"That's the strangest thing about it. The system has clearly been reprogrammed recently, but all earlier settings have been lost. It would be like starting from scratch. I could do it, but it would be several days' work, and I wouldn't like to guarantee that the results would be what you wanted. You would be far better off speaking to the expert who set it up!"

As the disconsolate membership left the building, the Irritable Witch of the South and the Unpleasant Witch of the North were seen dancing a jig around the parking lot, cackling uncontrollably.

The Power and the Glory

There was a sense of foreboding in the Club. For four weeks now, they had been forced to play in a nearby hotel, due to the mysterious malfunctioning of the air-conditioning system in the Club premises. The members were on tenterhooks awaiting the outcome of an emergency committee meeting.

The Wicked Witch of the West, the one member who understood how the system worked, had returned to town from an extended holiday and had found two committee members on her doorstep to ensure that her invitation to the meeting was delivered and accepted.

The meeting had begun at five o'clock with the intention of finishing ahead of the evening's bridge. As the clock ticked on towards seven and the scheduled start of play, the intended partners of the occupied committee members were eyeing each other up nervously. If the meeting went on, they would be left partnerless. Some wouldn't mind that, except that they would feel obliged to pair up with one of the other abandoned partners. On all the minds bar one, the main question was how to get paired up with almost anyone before the Unpleasant Witch of the North asked them. She was due to play with the Wicked Witch of the West that evening.

Just in time, at 6:58, the door to the committee room opened and Dorothy's Auntie Em emerged, her face glowering, her manner threatening, and everything about her showing she was just holding her temper and no more. A crowd of eager faces gathered round her, but quickly dispersed when they assessed her mood. Auntie Em was not a person to cross when things were going well, never mind when they were going badly. Uncle Henry alone was spoken to, and that was just to order him to get her a cup of coffee and a slice of fruit cake.

"Yes, rosebud," he said, accepting the order, as always.

The Honorary Chairman of the Lollipop Guild, looking grim, muttered that there would be no announcement at this point, and the committee members joined their partners.

The play began only five minutes late. Uncle Henry and six other players sat opposite grim, tight-lipped partners. The Unpleasant Witch of the North had an unusual problem. Her partner was so elated that even she couldn't find a way to upset her.

For once, no one seemed interested in the inadequacies of partners and the misdeeds of opponents. The Wicked Witch of the West was almost the only topic on anyone's lips, though the committee members maintained an ominous silence. Opinions varied between those who were hoping that she would be read the Riot Act and more vindictive members, who were looking for a ritual execution during the tea break.

The exception was the Scarecrow. Like so much of life, the workings of the club were above his head — a subject that seemed pointless to try to master when there were so many more important unsolved mysteries.

The Lion had been met with the disturbing news that in an attempt to improve his game, the Scarecrow had been reading again. They started the night against the Tin Man and Dorothy.

"Tell me," the Scarecrow began as he searched for his latest lucky pen, "what sort of leads do you think are best? I understand that the Ruritanian team has had some spectacular successes recently with coded eights and sixes."

"The answer to that is quite simple," said the Tin Man with an air of authority. "The best leads are intelligent ones based on listening to the auction, looking at your hand, and following a method agreed with your partner."

"Humph," said the Lion. "The best leads are ones that beat contracts. That's even simpler!"

"Very droll," began the Tin Man. But the discussion was cut short by an announcement from the tournament director. Play began, and sorting his cards, the Lion saw:

♠ A 7   ♡ J 10 9 6 4 3   ◇ K 9 4   ♣ A Q

The Scarecrow opened One Diamond, and after a pass by Dorothy, the Lion responded with One Heart. When the Scarecrow raised him to Three Hearts, the Lion's natural instinct was just to bid game. Playing against the Tin Man, however, he knew that if the slam were on, he would never hear the end of it if he failed to make a try. His Four Club cuebid was met with a Four Diamond cuebid from his partner. Reluctantly, he felt he had to go on and cuebid Four Spades.

The Scarecrow now bid Four Notrump. The Lion sighed inwardly. He had agreed to teach the Scarecrow Roman Keycard Blackwood, but the results to date seemed close to random. One more disaster and he would abandon the experiment. Still, he had to see it through on this hand. Apart from anything else, if he passed the Scarecrow would be declarer. With a known ten-card fit, he showed his two keycards and the equivalent of the queen of trumps by bidding Five Spades. The Scarecrow wasn't entirely sure what his partner's bid meant: was it three or six of the five aces? The safest thing seemed to be to put him into Six Hearts. That ended the auction.

The Tin Man led the ♡5 and the Lion, who generally needed some persuading to get as high as game, saw the dummy for his slam.

♠ K 3
♡ K 8 7 2
◇ A Q 6 5 3
♣ K J

♠ A 7
♡ J 10 9 6 4 3
◇ K 9 4
♣ A Q

Obviously, there were no side losers and the only question was how to play trumps. If Dorothy had both the ace and queen. then it didn't matter what he did. Good as he was, the Tin Man couldn't actually see through the backs of the cards and was highly unlikely to have led away from the queen. If he had led from A5 doubleton, then he was about to find out what a mistake he had made, for without the lead, the Lion's natural line would have been to run the jack. He called for the king in the hope and expectation of seeing the singleton queen come down. He sank back in his seat, deflated, when Dorothy discarded a club. An unbreakable contract had been broken. This was the full hand.

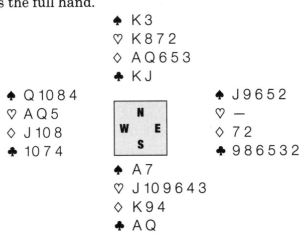

"What sort of lead was that?" spluttered the Lion. "Okay, it was the lead that beat the contract, but only because I didn't play you for being insane!"

"On the contrary," said the Tin Man. "It was an intelligent lead made by listening to the bidding and looking at my hand. With my strength, it was clear to me that Dorothy would hold very little in the way of high cards and was probably void in hearts. With my diamond holding, it was clear that dummy's suit was breaking. With your cuebids, it was very likely that your two keycards were the black aces. The odds were therefore very much in favor of finding the king of hearts in the dummy, and Trick 1 was obviously the best time to make you guess the suit. And even if you had held the king of hearts, what of it? My ace and queen would still have taken tricks at some point." Turning to Dorothy, he added, "Feel free to congratulate me."

"Sorry, I was waiting until we had a bigger audience," she replied dryly.

The tournament reached its midway point and the director announced that the normal tea break would be extended to thirty minutes, as the committee wished to reconvene.

The Chairman looked around at the seven other members of the committee and addressed the tournament. "Ladies and gentlemen, ladies and gentlemen, earlier, the committee agreed to have a break to let tempers cool, but we must now come to a conclusion. We will be back with you as soon as possible."

Uncle Henry was already on his way to pick up pots of tea and coffee and a plate of cookies.

Earlier, unabashed by outnumbering her opponents by one to seven, the Wicked Witch had skillfully held her assailants at bay. She had denied having tampered with the settings of the system. She was as bewildered as everyone else about the loss of the manual and the wiping out of the pre-programmed defaults. She could not account for the system failing just when she went on holiday.

She hadn't had this much fun in years.

Only very slowly had she allowed her motivation to appear through oblique hints. It had not occurred to anyone that the key to the mystery lay in the club constitution. Indeed, few of the members had given much thought to the approaching club

AGM, other than a vague wish to be able to hold it on their own premises. Fewer still had ever read the constitution.

The committee worked on a rotation basis. Members were limited to two consecutive three-year terms and then had to take a break for at least one term. For most of the souls willing to commit themselves to this thankless task, a chance to get off the committee felt like getting parole, but not for all. This year, the Wicked Witch of the West was coming to the end of her second term and had made it clear to all that she was not happy about the loss of status that she was about to incur.

"Perhaps she believes that she has immunity from prosecution while in office," the Tin Man had quipped.

The thirty minutes came and went. The tension levels were growing higher in the committee room. Inadvertently tapping her fingers on the last biscuit, the Wicked Witch shrugged her shoulders and gave a low chortle.

"This problem is as much of a mystery to me as it is to all of you."

"Be that as it may, be that as it may, you will not deny that you are our expert on the system, and we really need you to sort it out," the Honorary Chairman of the Lollipop Guild said pointedly.

"Oh, you are so kind. I didn't realize I was so highly thought of and so important to the Club." Even her attempts to look mournful had a certain glee about them. "I could have a look, but who am I to say if I will be able to improve the situation? This is a big responsibility, and of course I would only have a short time in which to try before I leave the committee. Obviously, the person in charge of this has to be a committee member. It is so central to the smooth running of the Club. By the way, which of you will be taking over from me as building convener when I shuffle off to retirement?"

There was an awkward silence.

"I mean, there is so much to be passed on. Never mind the air conditioning — who is going to take charge if there were problems with the electricity or," she paused for effect, "the plumbing?"

The committee members gasped. Auntie Em pulled herself up in her chair and spoke directly to the Wicked Witch.

"This is blackmail, and we will not stand for it. I don't care what schemes you have prepared to use against us. Anyone who would set out to ruin the Club has no place being a member of it."

"Tee hee hee! Blackmail is such an ugly word, especially when all I was doing was pointing out that for six years you have left me to sort out everything. Can I help it if I have become indispensable?"

"So what do you want? We are not changing the constitution to suit you," said Auntie Em with cold steel in her voice.

"Hee hee, of course not. Like everyone here, I want the Club to carry on as successfully as possible." She cackled. "I have a proposal to make...."

Meanwhile, in the playing area, the Tin Man had been taking the opportunity of the extended tea break to scribble on six sheets of paper. He strode across the bar towards Dorothy, the Lion, and the Scarecrow. He had the sort of look on his face that meant he had something very clever to tell them. The Lion sighed, but realized that there was no escape. The Tin Man handed each of them a piece of paper with a pair of hands neatly written on it.

♠ K 10
♡ A Q 3
◇ K 5 4 3 2
♣ Q J 2

♠ A Q 9 7 2
♡ K 10 6
◇ A 7
♣ A K 5

Without any opening pleasantries, the Tin Man launched into his speech. "Our discussion earlier reminded me of this hand from last week. South opens Two Notrump, then shows five spades. After checking that they aren't off an ace, North lunges into Seven Notrump. Not the best contract you have ever been in, but by no means the worst. How do you play it?"

"I think you have forgotten something," said Dorothy. "Before we do any playing, West has to make a lead."

"Quite right," said the Tin Man with an air of smug satisfaction. "To make it easier, I'll let you choose the lead and see if that helps."

The Lion growled apprehensively. "Well, you have eight sure tricks outside spades. Maybe you could squeeze someone in spades and diamonds if the spades don't break."

"Indeed you might, but to return to Dorothy's point, what lead would you like to receive?"

"Well, a spade, obviously. That will pick up the suit for me, give me four spades for sure, and probably five."

"Do go on," the Tin Man replied, trying, not very hard, to suppress a grin.

"Well, it's obvious isn't it?" snarled the Lion. "On a spade lead, I can play the ten as a free finesse, winning when West has the jack and picking up East's jack if he has it!"

"Is that what you would do?" asked the Tin Man.

"Yes! Get to the point!"

The Tin Man's face contorted into what people guessed was his take on a smile. "Yes, just like the declarer who held this hand, you get the lead of your dreams and then go down in a contract you would otherwise have made." He gave them each a second handout with the full deal.

```
              ♠ K 10
              ♡ A Q 3
              ◇ K 5 4 3 2
              ♣ Q J 2
♠ 8 6 5 4 3              ♠ J
♡ J 9 5       ┌─────────┐   ♡ 8 7 4 2
◇ Q 9         │    N    │   ◇ J 10 8 6
♣ 10 7 4      │  W   E  │   ♣ 9 8 6 3
              │    S    │
              └─────────┘
              ♠ A Q 9 7 2
              ♡ K 10 6
              ◇ A 7
              ♣ A K 5
```

"If the opponents lead any other suit, then you will obviously win that and before long set about spades. Obviously, you will lead a spade to the king, the jack will fall, and you will claim thirteen tricks. By playing the ten, you then need to use the ace or queen on the first round, resulting in West's eight controlling the suit.

"Now, you argue, quite reasonably," he continued in lecturing mode, "that since I allowed you to nominate the lead, West could have had any spade holding. Clearly, had he held Jxxx, playing the ten would have been a winning move. At the table, of course West was under no compulsion. He had heard the bidding and had chosen to lead a spade.

"Let us consider the holdings in which your play will make any difference. That is, if West holds Jxxx or if he holds two small. Now, would a sentient West consider leading from Jxxx into declarer's known five-card suit? It is inconceivable. No, West was clearly trying to find a neutral lead, and given his spade holding, this looked like the suit where he was least likely to blow a trick. That really rules out the possibility of him leading from two small either, a suit that he knows is not breaking. So, we are left with distributions where your play in spades will make no difference, or this particular one, in which it must be right to go up with the king. It just so happens that West inadvertently gave us an opportunity to take a losing option." The Tin Man sat back and cracked his knuckles. "It is up to us to turn the opportunity down."

"So are you going to claim that West was some sort of genius?" growled the Lion, crumpling both sheets into a ball.

"No, not really. As a wise man once said, sometimes the best leads are just those that happen to beat the contract."

Behind the Tin Man, a door opened, and for the second time that evening, seven grim faces and one gleeful figure emerged from the small room the committee had commandeered. The reconvened meeting had lasted for nearly an hour, and all outside had been treated to a chorus of complaints from the Unpleasant Witch of the North about how late she would be getting home.

The Honorary Chairman of the Lollipop Guild pulled himself up to his full four feet two inches. Taking a spoon from a nearby saucer, he banged it on a table to ensure he had everybody's attention — quite unnecessarily, as the whole room was focused on him.

"I am pleased to be able to tell you, yes, yes, very pleased to be able to tell you, that we expect to be back on our premises from next Monday. Our new facilities manager feels confident that all problems can be resolved by then."

There was silence. No one could think of what to say. They were delighted to go back to their club, but the Cheshire Cat face of the Wicked Witch told them all who the new facilities manager was.

As they went back to their table, Dorothy cornered Auntie Em. "What is going on?" she whispered.

"That woman had us over a barrel. We had no option. She's the devil, incarnate, she's ..." Auntie Em was blunt, but out of principle never swore. She was sorely tested.

"What does facilities manager mean?" said Dorothy, bravely venturing a second question.

"It means that that woman is permanently on the committee, and," Auntie Em spluttered, "she'll get paid an honorarium of 1,000 guilders a year."

"Well," Dorothy said to the Tin Man at the end of what had been a very long evening, "tonight has been all about leads. There was that trump lead you found against the Lion, and there was the hand you showed us at the interval. However, neither is on a par with the way the Wicked Witch of the West has managed to lead the committee and the whole Club by the nose!"

Dorothy silently vowed revenge.

7

There's No Place Like Home

Everyone was glad that the Club was back on its own premises. Even the hotel that had given them temporary residence saw their departure with a certain sense of relief. This was especially true of the bar staff. They had at first found the lingo and behavior of the Club members difficult to comprehend. However, they had quickly learned that "Let me give you a hand" was not an offer of help. Quite the opposite. Indeed, George and Manuel, neither of whom could distinguish a club from a spade, had become expert sympathizers. Manuel was particularly sought out by members in distress, his limited English being a distinct asset.

The Club was looking its best that April. The Wicked Witch of the West, now facilities manager, had done a great job. In addition to sorting out the malfunctioning air conditioning system, she had also arranged spring cleaning for the whole place. She had made the executive decision to hire some help for this, fortunately finding herself able to recruit some of her friends and relations. While wincing at the amount the Club had to pay, Auntie Em at least felt she had beaten the Wicked Witch down by pointing out that sales tax could be added only by officially registered companies.

The AGM this year was a formality. No one dared to mention the main subject on everyone's mind — the machinations of the Wicked Witch of the West. All of the major office bearers agreed to carry on in harness. Two Munchkins, who had had their arms twisted to stand, were elected to replace those who had completed their terms of office. Prizes were presented and applauded with all the heartfelt enthusiasm of an audience of losing Oscar nominees. It had been an especially good year for the Tin Man and Dorothy, who had won all of the main competitions.

Preliminaries out of the way, the most nerve-racking moment of the night arrived. It had long been the tradition at the club that after the official proceedings, those present drew for partners and played a short matchpoint game of around sixteen to twenty boards. There was a sigh of relief all round, not least from the Tin Man himself, when he drew Dorothy. Not everyone was so lucky. Uncle Henry was going to have to relive his worst session of the previous season, playing with the Scarecrow. The Wicked Witch of the West found herself paired up with Auntie Em and starting against Dorothy and the Tin Man.

On finding out their draw, Auntie Em made straight for the West seat, hoping to irritate her partner. The Wicked Witch, however, just gave a gap-toothed grin.

"Trying to see things from my point of view. How considerate of you!"

Auntie Em turned her attention to the Tin Man. Taking his trophies off the table, she said, "What were the odds of that?"

"What? Me winning all the main events? Well, if you look at my record over the years, then I would calculate them as..." The silverware itself was actually of little interest to the Tin Man. As long as his name was on it.

"No, not that. The odds of you drawing Dorothy tonight? Shame for her, poor girl. And anyway, if you want to talk about main trophies, how often have you won the Ladies Afternoon Friendly Summer League?"

Dorothy tried to change the subject. "I see the Lion is playing with your farmhand, Zeke. They should be well-matched, and they shouldn't run into any time problems. They're both so conservative that they will probably pass out half of the boards."

Auntie Em and the Wicked Witch of the West disdained to discuss methods, not even their notrump range, and the Tin Man was disappointed when they left his table with what was likely to be a couple of averages.

Dorothy and the Tin Man's next opponents were the Mayor of Munchkinland and the Unpleasant Witch of the North. The Mayor was not the best player in the Club, but he knew how to please his constituency and allowed his partner to play both of the hands.

Their third opponents were the Scarecrow and Uncle Henry. Dorothy could hear the apologetic tone of the Scarecrow's voice before she could make out the words.

"You must admit that I was unlucky on that hand," he was saying as they sat down. "A 4-3 split is sixty-two percent. I have been memorizing the percentages, as I am sure it must help my game, and I do so want to improve."

Uncle Henry snorted. "Percentages? I can't see why you bother with such advanced mathematics when you haven't got the hang of adding yet. The chance of a 4-3 split doesn't matter much when you are missing eight cards in the suit."

"But you had — "

"Quiet, quiet," interrupted the Tin Man. "We may still have to play the hand."

"Not in the contract we played it," Uncle Henry said, scowling, "and certainly not on the same line of play."

"Anyway," said the Tin Man. "Percentages are not enough by themselves. They need to be applied, and modified, within the context of the given hand."

Dorothy, South, was the dealer with both sides vulnerable. Playing their usual weak notrump, she opened One Notrump holding:

♠872 ♡A865 ◇J1083 ♣AK

West	North	East	South
Uncle H	Tin Man	Scarecrow	Dorothy
			1NT
pass	2♣	pass	2♡
pass	4♡	all pass	

After Stayman from her partner, she showed her hearts. The
Tin Man raised her to Four Hearts and Uncle Henry led the ◇6.
The Tin Man carefully laid out his cards in the usual perfect
straight lines. Dorothy could see:

♠ A K Q J
♡ K J 9 2
◇ 9 7 2
♣ 6 4

♠ 8 7 2
♡ A 8 6 5
◇ J 10 8 3
♣ A K

The Scarecrow won with the queen and followed it with the
ace and king, Uncle Henry throwing an encouraging club on
the third round. The Scarecrow looked at dummy briefly, then
switched to the ♣J. Dorothy played the ace and considered
her prospects. The fate of the contract obviously depended on
playing trumps for no loser. If there was a singleton queen or
ten in the Scarecrow's hand, she could pick up a 4-1 break. The
obvious thing to do seemed to be to play the ♡A, then finesse
the jack. It wasn't a bad contract, she mused, though it would
have been a lot better with nine trumps between them.

Suddenly, it occurred to her that Uncle Henry might not
know that she didn't have a club loser; perhaps he could be
persuaded to move the odds in her favor? She put the ◇J on
the table. Sure enough, her uncle ruffed, with the four. She
over-ruffed and played a heart to the ace, the Scarecrow con-

tributing the three and Uncle Henry the seven. When she continued with a heart towards dummy, Uncle Henry played the ten. Decision time. Would Uncle Henry have ruffed so readily holding Q10xx of trumps? Probably not. She called for the king and was pleased to see the queen drop.

This was the full hand:

Dealer South. Both vul.

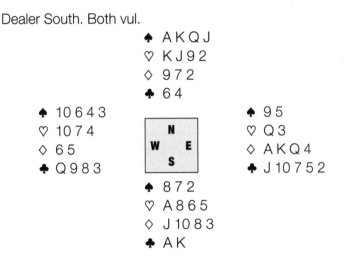

```
                    ♠ A K Q J
                    ♡ K J 9 2
                    ◇ 9 7 2
                    ♣ 6 4
   ♠ 10 6 4 3                        ♠ 9 5
   ♡ 10 7 4          N               ♡ Q 3
   ◇ 6 5          W     E            ◇ A K Q 4
   ♣ Q 9 8 3         S               ♣ J 10 7 5 2
                    ♠ 8 7 2
                    ♡ A 8 6 5
                    ◇ J 10 8 3
                    ♣ A K
```

"Well played, partner," said the Tin Man. "You see, Henry, Scarecrow: had Dorothy taken the percentage line missing queen-ten to five trumps, she would have gone down. Instead, she arranged, thanks to you, Henry, to be missing queen-ten to four trumps, which gave her a much better chance of success."

"What do you mean, thanks to me?" growled Uncle Henry. "How could I know she wasn't going to throw a club loser?"

"Ah, that would be going back to arithmetic. You presumed the Scarecrow held the king of clubs. What, then, was Dorothy's hand for her One Notrump? The ace and queen of hearts, jack of diamonds and ace of clubs are the only available honor cards and they only come to eleven points. Most important of all, even if she had decided to open that hand One Notrump, she would not have played the hand that way but would have drawn trumps before taking her discard."

In the bar afterwards, the Lion was looking at his scoresheet, pleased to see a succession of plus scores.

"We should be quite good," he said to Zeke. "Plus scores are what you want at matchpoint scoring."

"Very true," said the Tin Man, looking over his shoulder, "But I'm not sure that applies to plus scores of 170, 190, and 210. Anyway, what's that -150 there on Board 6, where game is cold your way?"

The hand in question had elicited the Tin Man's second "well played, partner" of the evening, much to Dorothy's astonishment. Interestingly, it was a different variation on the theme of dealing with queen to five in a key suit.

The Lion had played the hand against Uncle Henry and the Scarecrow, while Dorothy was in the South seat with the Honorary Chairman of the Lollipop Guild on her right. The Chairman had assured himself of a pleasant evening in which he was unlikely to face the embarrassment of having to present himself with a prize by drawing Glinda, the Good Witch.

Both the Lion and Dorothy found themselves declaring Three Notrump after opening the South hand Two Notrump.

Dealer East. EW vul.

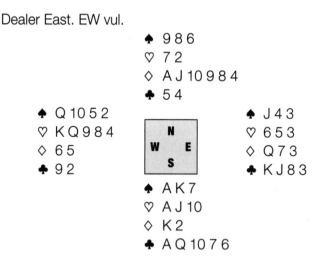

Both Wests led the ♡K. Both Norths laid down dummy. The Tin Man commented on partner needing a perfect fit to make Six Diamonds a good contract, while Zeke apologized for the rush of blood that had caused him to bid game.

"The very best of luck, partner. If these diamonds are no good to you, then this could be pretty dicey."

The Lion nodded his head, his mane of golden hair bouncing, and fixed his attention on the best way to play this key suit. He laid down the ◇K and followed up with the ◇2. When West played low to the second round, he sat for a minute, crouched over his cards. Eventually, he called for the jack — "Playing the percentages," as he later defended himself. East won the queen and returned a heart. The Lion's jack was allowed to score and he switched to ace and another club. The defense took their three heart tricks and switched to spades. Declarer was held to an embarrassing six tricks: two spades, two hearts, and one trick in each minor.

"The hand was a death trap," he announced. "No way to pick up the diamonds, and the clubs don't break. I could have saved a trick by going up with the ace of diamonds. You really needed a few more points to raise me to game. A suit like that is all very well, but it needs an outside entry." Zeke knew better than to suggest that going up with the ◇A might have saved two tricks, as then a successful club finesse could have been taken.

After the same lead, Dorothy did her thinking a trick earlier than the Lion. She considered the merit of playing off the top two diamonds, trying to drop a doubleton queen in either hand, then turning to clubs if diamonds had not come in. Shame she didn't have an extra entry to the dummy to lead clubs twice. Then it came to her that she wouldn't mind losing a diamond finesse, as long as it was on the first round! She would be able to win any return and overtake the ◇K. If the finesse won, then she would have the extra entry she wanted to play on clubs.

She put the ◇2 on the table and called for the jack. The Honorary Chairman of the Lollipop Guild viewed this suspiciously. If his partner had started with ◇Kx, then it was vital that he duck, and he could remonstrate with her, in a kindly way, for not putting the king in. He allowed the jack to win and Dorothy switched to clubs, putting in the ten. When that scored, she overtook the ◇K with dummy's ace and played a second club. When the queen held, she cashed the ace and set up the long club, giving her ten tricks before the defense could do more than score a heart, a diamond, and a club.

"Well played, again," said the Tin Man.

"Well-played" from the Tin Man twice in one night, thought Dorothy. I wonder what percentage chance that is?

8

Defense of the Realm

The Club's handicap teams had attracted twelve entries. Last year's winners, Dorothy, the Tin Man, the Lion and the Scarecrow, had started with a bye, and then qualified for the semifinal by beating a team of Munchkins. Starting from a handicap of 50 IMPs, the Tin Man, probably justifiably, reckoned that he and Dorothy had pulled in three times that deficit. The Lion had been close to a panic attack each time they had scored up, as it had been one of the Scarecrow's off-days: his on-days were worrying enough. The final margin of 3 IMPs may have been beyond the comprehension of the Tin Man, but came as a great relief to the Lion. The Tin Man had referred at least five times since the match to the partscore hand where he and Dorothy had taken 1100 and had lost 12 IMPs.

They were matched up in the semifinal against Dorothy's Auntie Em and Uncle Henry and a couple of their farmhands, Zeke and Hickory. This foursome had also enjoyed a bye in the first round, and their previous round against the team of the Honorary Chairman of the Lollipop Guild was one that three of the team wanted expunged from their collective memories. Conceding a handicap of 25 IMPs, Zeke had been struck down with a stomach bug a few hours before the match. There had been no option but to recruit the only reserve available, Hank the Hunk.

The primary reason for Hank being available was that the handicap system in use didn't go high enough to compensate for having him on the team of any sensible captain. Auntie Em decided she would play with him and sent "the boys" to the other table with instructions to bid game on any hand where there might be the slightest chance of making it.

She then presented Hank with a very simple convention card, which she described as modified Acol, and assured him it was the latest idea, having been actively developed by the Uzbekistani Open Team. It was based on six-card majors and transfer openings by him. When Auntie Em was the opener they played four-card majors and transfer responses by him.

The system worked as it was intended to. Auntie Em played fourteen of the twenty-four hands, twelve of them in Three Notrump. Her success rate wasn't as high as it might have been in normal play, but it was sufficient for them to scrape through by 2 IMPs. Hank was very impressed. He wasn't used to being on a winning team and resolved to see if there were any books on this Uzbek system, so that he could study it in more detail at his leisure.

As in the previous rounds, this semifinal match was to be played in four sets of six boards, switching opponents after each set.

"So, how is your defense of the trophy going?" asked Auntie Em as the players readied themselves. "They really whacked your handicap up this year."

"So far so good," said the Tin Man. "Our handicap is just the same as always; I think he'll be sitting East this set."

Auntie Em won the toss and elected to put the farmhands in against Dorothy and the Tin Man in the odd-numbered sets, facing them herself in the crucial last set.

With Dorothy's team having 20 IMPs to make up, they were hoping for some action. The deals seemed disappointingly quiet. They came to the last board of the set, and Dorothy found herself as declarer on a partscore hand:

Dealer South. N/S vul.

```
              ♠ 8 3
              ♡ A 5 2
              ◇ 10 8 4
              ♣ Q J 9 6 2
              ┌──────────┐
              └──────────┘
              ♠ A Q 10 9 7
              ♡ Q 7
              ◇ A J 6 5
              ♣ 5 4
```

West	North	East	South
Zeke	Tin Man	Hickory	Dorothy
			1♠
pass	1NT	pass	2◇
pass	2♠	all pass	

Zeke, in the West seat, led the ♣3.

Dorothy called for the ♣J and East won with the ace. He switched to a heart. Dorothy tried the queen and took West's king with her ace. In dummy for probably the last time, she ran the ♠8 and was pleasantly surprised when it held the trick. Continuing with the dummy's last trump, she took the jack with the queen and cashed the ace, drawing the outstanding trumps.

Dorothy could see seven tricks now — five trumps and two aces. Lacking anything better to do, she led her remaining club towards the entryless dummy. West won with the king and played the ♡J and another heart. Dorothy ruffed and led a diamond towards the dummy. West played low and she tried the eight, hoping to draw an honor. Unfortunately, East won the nine. He played a fourth heart, Dorothy ruffed with her last trump, and West threw a club. Disconsolately, she played the ace and another diamond hoping that whoever won it would have to give dummy the ♣Q at Trick 13. Instead, West claimed the two top diamonds.

"Tut tut," said the Tin Man. "You had it made."

This had been the full hand:

Dealer South. N/S vul.

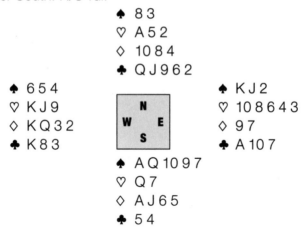

```
                    ♠ 8 3
                    ♡ A 5 2
                    ◇ 10 8 4
                    ♣ Q J 9 6 2
    ♠ 6 5 4                          ♠ K J 2
    ♡ K J 9          N               ♡ 10 8 6 4 3
    ◇ K Q 3 2     W     E            ◇ 9 7
    ♣ K 8 3          S               ♣ A 10 7
                    ♠ A Q 10 9 7
                    ♡ Q 7
                    ◇ A J 6 5
                    ♣ 5 4
```

Since they were waiting for the other table to finish, all three of the participants were treated to the Tin Man's post-mortem.

"Fancy getting a three-card ending wrong."

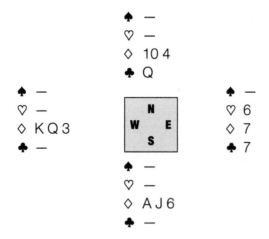

```
                    ♠ —
                    ♡ —
                    ◇ 10 4
                    ♣ Q
    ♠ —                                ♠ —
    ♡ —              N                 ♡ 6
    ◇ K Q 3       W     E              ◇ 7
    ♣ —              S                 ♣ 7
                    ♠ —
                    ♡ —
                    ◇ A J 6
                    ♣ —
```

"All you have to do is play a small diamond and West is endplayed. Your line would only work if one defender, which would have to be West, was left with king-queen doubleton of diamonds and the last club, as otherwise the defense would be able to arrange for East to win the diamond exit and cash the last heart. Indeed, if he had that exact holding, you would still have made by exiting with a small diamond at Trick 11, as he would have had to play back a diamond to your ace-jack or a club to dummy's queen." He shook his head. "Very sloppy. I fear your aunt may well make this one, so we'll lose 5 IMPs we can scarcely spare."

Dorothy considered mentioning East's failure to cover the ♠8 but saw no benefit in embarrassing him, and there was no knowing whether the Scarecrow would be up to it anyway.

A knock on the door signaled that the other table had finished. The Lion had a face like thunder as he and the Scarecrow came in. Muttering something about "one lousy bad lead," the Lion sat down and started to read out his scores. After five boards, they were leading by 4 IMPs to 1. The Lion pushed his scoresheet towards the Tin Man, who read, "Minus 130? How on earth did you allow them to make ten tricks in clubs or diamonds? That's 6 IMPs away."

"Not ten tricks, not in a minor, one lousy bad lead," the Lion growled.

The Tin Man went metallic grey as he whispered, "Minus 1130! Three Spades doubled made eleven! What happened?"

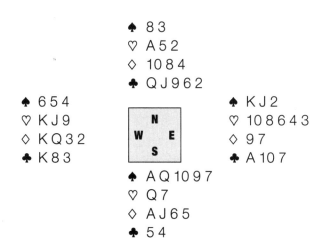

It had transpired that over Auntie Em's One Spade opening, the Lion had put in a double. Uncle Henry had bid One Notrump and the Scarecrow had bid Two Hearts. Not easily put off, Auntie Em had forged ahead with Two Spades. After a quick pass from the Lion, and a slow one from Uncle Henry, the Scarecrow had pressed on with Three Hearts. After two passes, Uncle Henry took the push to Three Spades, which the Scarecrow doubled.

Trying to give nothing away, the Lion had led a trump to the king and ace. Auntie Em tried a club to the jack and the Scarecrow's ace. He switched to a diamond, and Auntie Em ducked to the Lion's queen.

The Lion was worried. He could see potential danger in every suit. Not wishing to finesse his partner's trumps again, to give away a diamond trick, or to set up dummy's clubs, he tried a heart away from his king — after all, his partner had bid them twice. Auntie Em ran that to her queen and played her second club from hand. Hoping that she would mis-guess and put in the nine, the Lion played low. In view of the Lion's double of One Spade, Auntie Em went up with the queen. When she played dummy's ♠8, the Scarecrow played low, and she put in the seven from hand, retaining the lead in dummy. Next came the third round of clubs, ruffed in hand, bringing down the king. The ♠Q drew the trumps and the ♡A was still in dummy as an entry for dummy's established clubs. Having lost only one club and one diamond, that came to eleven tricks.

"One lousy bad lead! Yes, and how! And three rotten bids! And about eight misdefenses!" screeched the Tin Man. "And most of that from the West seat," he concluded, coldly glaring at the Lion.

The net result was a loss of 15 IMPs on the board. They entered the second quarter trailing by 32 IMPs.

The next set started hopefully for Dorothy's team. Auntie Em over-reached to a couple of non-making thin games. Dorothy felt confident that the cowardly Lion would be unlikely to look at either of them. The Tin Man had doubled the second one and picked up a useful-looking 500.

On the next hand, the Tin Man held:

♠ K 10 9 5   ♡ 8 7 5 4 2   ◊ 5   ♣ A K 2

With neither side vulnerable, he heard Auntie Em open One Diamond on his right. Liking his shape, he tried a takeout double. Uncle Henry's Two Notrump response showed a sound raise to at least Three Diamonds. Dorothy chipped in with Three Clubs and Auntie Em, a lover of short auctions, finished the bidding with a trademark jump to game — Five Diamonds on this occasion. The full auction had been:

West	North	East	South
Tin Man	Uncle H	Dorothy	Auntie Em
			1◊
dbl	2NT	3♣	5◊
all pass			

The Tin Man led the ♣A and when dummy came down, this was the position he could see:

```
                    ♠ 8 6 3 2
                    ♡ Q J
                    ◊ K Q J 8 2
                    ♣ 5 4
    ♠ K 10 9 5
    ♡ 8 7 5 4 2        N
    ◊ 5            W       E
    ♣ A K 2           S
```

Dorothy dropped the ♣Q under the ace. Auntie Em ruffed the club continuation and played a trump to dummy's king. When both opponents followed, it was clear from Auntie Em's demeanor that this had completed the task of drawing trumps.

Declarer's next move was to play three rounds of hearts. Dummy's queen won the first round, and then Auntie Em overtook the jack with the king and played the ace, discarding a spade. With Dorothy following to all three rounds, the distribution of the hands was an open book to the Tin Man. At this stage he could see:

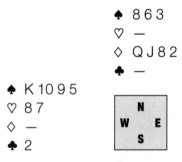

```
              ♠ 8 6 3
              ♡ —
              ◊ Q J 8 2
              ♣ —
♠ K 10 9 5         ┌─────────┐
♡ 8 7             │    N    │
◊ —               │  W   E  │
♣ 2               │    S    │
                  └─────────┘
```

While Auntie Em contemplated her next move, the Tin Man checked his logic. Dorothy was known to have started with seven clubs, one diamond, and three hearts, so had to have a doubleton spade. Auntie Em must have started with a 3=3=6=1 distribution. If she had the ♠AQJ, then the defense would never get anything more than one spade trick to go with the ♣A. He had to hope she had something weaker.

Eventually, Auntie Em played the ♠A. The Tin Man and dummy played low and Dorothy played the queen.

Auntie Em continued with a small spade and the Tin Man was just about to win the trick cheaply with the nine when he stopped himself. If Dorothy had the ♠QJ doubleton, she was about to be thrown in and forced to concede a ruff and discard! Auntie Em was playing for a crocodile coup. What luck for his team that he had been the player in the right seat when this came up. With the degree of drama required of the situation, he placed the king on the table, ready for the acknowledgement of his audience. Dummy's six was played and Dorothy produced the seven. Not even trying to hide her grin, Auntie Em showed the ♠J and claimed the rest. This was the full hand:

Dealer South. Neither vul.

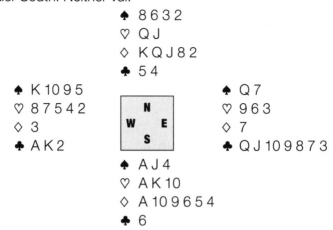

```
                    ♠ 8 6 3 2
                    ♡ Q J
                    ◇ K Q J 8 2
                    ♣ 5 4
  ♠ K 10 9 5                      ♠ Q 7
  ♡ 8 7 5 4 2          N          ♡ 9 6 3
  ◇ 3              W       E      ◇ 7
  ♣ A K 2              S          ♣ Q J 10 9 8 7 3
                    ♠ A J 4
                    ♡ A K 10
                    ◇ A 10 9 6 5 4
                    ♣ 6
```

"Good try," said Dorothy to the Tin Man. "I had to unblock the queen to avoid being endplayed."

"Good try, my foot," said Auntie Em. "You'll always play the queen in that situation and queen small was twice as likely as queen-jack. It's a sort of reverse restricted choice." She turned to the Tin Man. "I seem to recall I asked you how your defense was going and now I know the answer, whether you take it as the defense of the cup or in general."

The Tin Man looked stunned. He opened his mouth as if to issue a suitable riposte, but no words came out.

As it happened, the board didn't prove too costly. The Lion and the Scarecrow had doubled the opponents in Five Clubs for 300. In addition, they had one blunder that cost 10 IMPs but had gained on the hands where Auntie Em had overbid. The net result was that the set was a tie. With twelve boards to go, Dorothy's team still trailed by 32 IMPs.

All That Glitters

The Lion was enjoying the half-time coffee. He was also stoking up with several slices of cake to ready himself for the next six boards against Dorothy's Auntie Em. Actually, the thought of the play didn't bother him, but forty-five minutes later, they would be scoring up with the Tin Man. He could think of more pleasant ways to spend the time, such as getting several teeth extracted without anesthetic.

He was still smarting from the Three Spades doubled making two overtricks in the first set. Auntie Em was not a woman to leave a knife unused when there was a wound to twist it in. Before the Lion had even taken his seat, she began.

"Plus 1130, that's a score you don't see every day," she said, chuckling. "Not that you kids will see it today unless you take a gander at our scorecard."

Growling quietly, the Lion settled himself in the South seat and picked up his cards for the first board.

Dealer South. N/S vul.

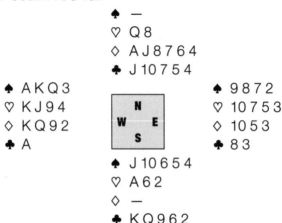

	♠ —	
	♡ Q 8	
	◊ A J 8 7 6 4	
	♣ J 10 7 5 4	
♠ A K Q 3		♠ 9 8 7 2
♡ K J 9 4		♡ 10 7 5 3
◊ K Q 9 2		◊ 10 5 3
♣ A		♣ 8 3
	♠ J 10 6 5 4	
	♡ A 6 2	
	◊ —	
	♣ K Q 9 6 2	

He opened One Club. He knew that some people would open One Spade, but he preferred to keep the auction low. Auntie Em and Uncle Henry played little in the way of a system, but to keep Uncle Henry happy, what they did play was firmly rooted in the 1950s or earlier. She made an old-fashioned Two Clubs cuebid to show a big hand.

The Scarecrow was unsure of how to deal with this situation. He was always encouraged to support when he had support. Not doing so risked annoying his partner and, if he ended up playing the hand, his teammates. In this case, the club could be short and there was only a limited chance of playing the hand if he bid a minor. He bid Two Diamonds.

Uncle Henry, rather relieved, passed.

The Lion didn't like the way the auction was developing. He had to bid and the obvious choice seemed to be Two Spades. Auntie Em happily doubled. The Scarecrow, knowing now that the Lion had clubs, decided to short-circuit the auction with a leap to Five Clubs. Auntie Em, a great fan of short and swift bidding sequences, particularly liked this one. Struggling to keep the smile from her face, she doubled again when the auction came around to her, anticipating a juicy penalty from her vulnerable opponents. The only regret was that the Lion would be playing the hand. The Scarecrow would have been worth an extra 300, at least.

Uncle Henry felt under pressure. He couldn't see much defense to this freely bid game and decided to pull to Five Hearts, confident that they had a fit and hoping that it would be cheap at the vulnerability. As soon as his bidding card touched the table, the look on Auntie Em's face told him he had done the wrong thing. The Lion and Auntie Em passed, and Uncle Henry trembled as he desperately tried to work out how he would explain his bid in the unlikely event that he managed to get a word in during the anticipated harangue.

Many aspects of the Scarecrow's game had been described politely as imperfect. Table presence, however, was one part of his game for which there was no polite description. He was completely unaware of the waves of hate passing from his right to his left. He too, could see little defense to the opposition contract. Trusting in the size of their club fit rather than their defense, which had already proved fragile that evening, he sacrificed in Six Clubs. After two passes, Auntie Em doubled with a crow of triumph that allowed no misinterpretation. The auction, a long one by Auntie Em's standards, was finally over.

West	North	East	South
Auntie Em	*Scarecrow*	*Uncle H*	*Lion*
			1♣
2♣	2◇	pass	2♠
dbl	5♣	pass	pass
dbl	pass	5♡	pass
pass	6♣	pass	pass
dbl	all pass		

Auntie Em slapped the ♠A on the table and the Scarecrow put down dummy with an incoherent, muttered apology. The Lion could see that Five Hearts would have been a slaughter on a spade lead. Trying to put that out of his mind, he looked for a way to limit the damage. It seemed to him that a crossruff would keep down his losses. He ruffed the opening lead, threw a heart on the ◇A, then ruffed backwards and forwards in spades and diamonds, reaching this position with the lead in dummy:

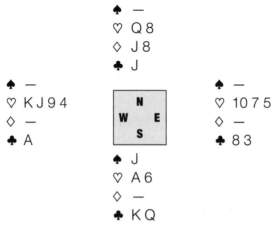

With the first eight tricks in the bag, he led a master diamond from the dummy. To prevent declarer from discarding a heart, Uncle Henry ruffed and the Lion overruffed. With her dreams of a four-figure penalty already shattered, Auntie Em was by now seriously worried. If she overruffed, she would be endplayed, forced to lead away from her ♡K, so she threw the ♡4.

The ♠J hit the table next. Auntie Em snorted. The Lion was giving the defense a ruff and discard, but, feeling powerless, she discarded a second heart as dummy ruffed. Down to the last three cards each, they held:

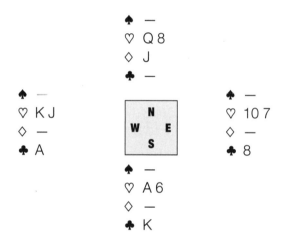

The Lion called for the ◇J, a second ruff and discard for the defense, but which, again, could do them no good. Uncle Henry ruffed and the Lion overruffed. Auntie Em was left helpless. Discarding a heart was obviously hopeless, so she overruffed and tried the ♡J. The Lion had the presence of mind to put in dummy's queen. Twelve tricks were his!

"You never know when to leave well alone, do you?" grumbled Uncle Henry.

Auntie Em was apoplectic. "Any sane person with twenty-two points and loads of defense would double Five Clubs. Only a lunatic would find that Five Heart bid!" Her explosion continued. "It would probably have been a flat board with Five

Clubs doubled making for 750 when you offered them at least 800 on a plate."

"Interesting that you don't anticipate them making an overtrick in Five Clubs," said Henry. "How can it possibly make apart from on a crossruff? Lead out your ace of trumps and take away two of their trumps, then watch declarer stew in that crazy slam."

The Lion leant forward. "Pardon me for interrupting this interesting analysis, but I don't happen to know the score for Six Clubs doubled making. I wonder if I could see it on your scorecard? In the minus column, of course," he purred.

Meanwhile, Dorothy was playing a contract at the other end of the scale.

Dealer North. Neither vul.

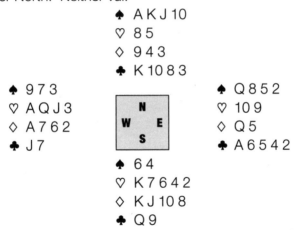

♠ A K J 10
♥ 8 5
♦ 9 4 3
♣ K 10 8 3

♠ 9 7 3
♥ A Q J 3
♦ A 7 6 2
♣ J 7

♠ Q 8 5 2
♥ 10 9
♦ Q 5
♣ A 6 5 4 2

♠ 6 4
♥ K 7 6 4 2
♦ K J 10 8
♣ Q 9

Zeke and Hickory, sitting North and South respectively, knew that every bid they made would be mercilessly analyzed at the end of the evening by Auntie Em. This served to reinforce their natural caution, and neither was tempted to make a light opening bid. Dorothy, sitting West, found the bidding passed around to her. After considering passing the hand out, she decided to open a weak notrump. Everybody passed. Zeke led the ♠A.

"Thanks," said Dorothy, "nice dummy."

After examining dummy's holding with slight disappointment, Zeke continued with the king and then the ten, South
discarding a discouraging heart. In dummy, Dorothy thought
she might as well take the heart finesse, and when it won, she
repeated it. North showed an even number, which, if true, had
to be two since the king hadn't appeared from South. Also, it
seemed quite likely that South would have thrown one from
king and four small.

Dorothy could now see six tricks: one spade, three hearts,
one diamond and one club. She had noted North's play of the
♠10 rather than the jack. This suggested that his entry to his
remaining spade winner was in clubs, and, as a passed hand,
that would rule out the possibility of him holding the ◇K. It
seemed that neither red suit provided much hope for a further
trick and dummy lacked the entries to set up clubs.

With no positive way forward herself, Dorothy decided to
see what could be developed if she handed the initiative to the
opposition. She led her small club and let it ride around to
South. Hickory, winning the trick with the nine, could see that
leading a red card would concede a trick, so he continued with
the ♣Q. Zeke, as North, saw the danger of his partner being
endplayed and covered it with the king. Dorothy called for the
ace, leaving this position:

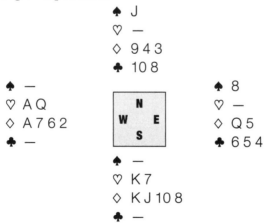

Dorothy began to see light at the end of the tunnel. She
led a club from the table. As expected, North won this and

proceeded to cash his other two black winners. As the last one was played, Dorothy followed suit from the dummy, turned to Hickory, and smiled. Down to 2-2 in the red suits, he had the unappetizing choice of which red king to bare.

"Well played," he said. "An unusual squeeze in that the threat was in an entryless hand."

Both tables had finished and the Lion came marching through with his chest puffed up as high as he could manage while still being able to breathe, desperate to tell his team-mates about his doubled slam. For once, the Tin Man was almost at a loss for words, but eventually he managed to say, "Very good card, very well done." The opposition lead had al-most been wiped out and they went into the final quarter just 5 IMPs behind, which put them right on schedule, as Dorothy observed.

For the last set, the Lion and the Scarecrow were back up against the two farmhands. Five of the boards proved to be depressingly dull and it was hard to see how the lead could have been reduced. Only one hand offered much of a chance of a swing.

Dealer South. Neither vul.

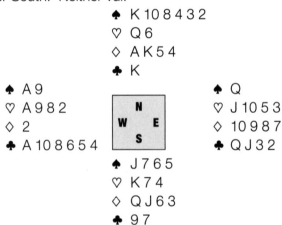

The bidding began with a One Club opening from West. The Scarecrow, sitting North, was about to overcall in spades when a thought struck him. The match was very close, and he didn't want to be declarer on what might be a critical hand. He doubled as a two-way option: he could always show his spade suit later, and with luck, his partner would bid something that he could raise.

It couldn't have worked out better. East responded One Heart, and then the Lion bid One Spade. After West raised to Two Hearts, the Scarecrow, euphoric at his good decision, raised to Four Spades, blissfully unaware that the bidding had seriously devalued two of his five honor cards. This ended the auction.

West	North	East	South
Zeke	Scarecrow	Hickory	Lion
			pass
1♣	dbl	1♡	1♠
2♡	4♠	all pass	

West led the ◊2, and it was clear to the Lion that this was a singleton.

The contract depended solely on keeping his trump losers to one. He led the ♠J towards the dummy and started to breathe heavily when the nine appeared. He was pretty sure that West would have the ace, so on that basis, his holding was either AQ9 or A9. If it was the former he should finesse, if it was the latter he should play the king. He could see no way of telling so decided to play the opener for the extra points and called for a small card in a low growl. When the queen appeared, his face fell. The defense cashed their three aces to take the contract one off.

"I'm sure old Tin Can Man will have some fancy reason for getting that right," the Lion muttered to himself.

Dorothy and the Tin Man were back up against Auntie Em and Uncle Henry, and this was their last board. It was clear to all four of them that the first five boards had been routine and all knew that the last hand, the replay of the Lion's Four Spades, was likely to be crucial.

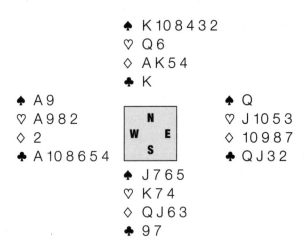

♠ K 10 8 4 3 2
♡ Q 6
♢ A K 5 4
♣ K

♠ A 9
♡ A 9 8 2
♢ 2
♣ A 10 8 6 5 4

♠ Q
♡ J 10 5 3
♢ 10 9 8 7
♣ Q J 3 2

♠ J 7 6 5
♡ K 7 4
♢ Q J 6 3
♣ 9 7

Uncle Henry passed as South and Dorothy opened One Club. Auntie Em didn't have the same misgivings as the Scarecrow and took the more normal action of overcalling One Spade. The Tin Man made a negative double, and Uncle Henry raised preemptively to Three Spades.

Dorothy saw that the value of her hand after her partner's double, almost guaranteeing that they had a fit in hearts, was far better than a count of her high-card points suggested. She bid Four Hearts. Auntie Em pressed on with Four Spades, taking the safe course, as it wasn't at all clear whose hand this was. The Tin Man and Uncle Henry both passed, leaving Dorothy with the crucial decision.

Had she set up a forcing pass situation by bidding Four Hearts? Probably not, but she wasn't sure. Were they beating Four Spades? Possibly, but she wasn't sure about that either — it certainly wouldn't be going down much. Could they make anything at the five-level? It was easy to give partner hands where Five Clubs or Five Hearts would be very good — partner didn't need many points as long as they were in the right places. Prepared for her partner's wrath if she was wrong, Dorothy bid Five Clubs. Everyone seemed to have bid themselves out because this was passed all around.

West	North	East	South
Dorothy	Auntie Em	Tin Man	Uncle H
			pass
1♣	1♠	dbl*	3♠
4♡	4♠	pass	pass
5♣	all pass		

Auntie Em led the ◇A and the Tin Man laid his hand down with a slight awkwardness.

"Not a classic," he confessed, "but at least I don't hold much defense."

Dorothy contented herself with "Thank you, partner," while wondering what he would have said if she had tabled this pile of dross.

Uncle Henry played an encouraging card, and Auntie Em continued with a second top diamond, which Dorothy ruffed. She had to hold her club and heart losers to a total of one. Ideally, she would like to run the ♣Q and take the double finesse in hearts, but dummy was rather short on entries. She could ruff a spade and take the club finesse. All being well, that would be covered by the king and she would then have an entry in the ♣J. That would allow her to take one heart finesse but, with only the ♣3 and ♣2 in dummy, she would not be able to get back to take another one, and would be forced to try to drop a doubleton honor.

The alternative was to play the ♣A. If either hand had the singleton king, then she would have two entries to the dummy to take the heart finesses. Yes, that seemed a better shot. Auntie Em was less than happy as she tossed her king onto the table.

Dorothy and the Tin Man returned to their teammates' table. The Lion glanced at their scorecard and his body slumped when he saw a game score on the final board, then puffed up when he saw that it was in their plus column.

"Don't worry," he said. "We talked them out of their Five Clubs."

"Well done," said Dorothy. "These advance sacrifices where you have more points than the opponents are not easy to judge."

The 9 IMPs that they gained on this board proved to be enough to see them through to the final by 2 IMPs. Zeke, Hickory and Uncle Henry came through to congratulate them, and Auntie Em, after a few minutes berating an empty table, grudgingly followed.

They were now set for the final, where they would meet their long-standing rivals: the witches.

 # The Bet

In the final, the Irritable Witch of the South would, as usual, be playing with the Unpleasant Witch of the North. The Wicked Witch of the West was partnering Glinda, the Good Witch. Reckoned in the witching profession to be among the most accomplished in her line of work, Glinda's skills did not transfer to bridge. Younger members of the Club couldn't understand why the other three witches, none of them famed for good nature or tolerance, accepted Glinda on their team. Older members remembered the late Eerie Witch of the East and the never-ending allegations of cheating. To them, it was clear Glinda had been brought in to provide an air of respectability.

The two sides were considered to be fairly close in ability. Irritable, Unpleasant and Wicked weren't quite in the technical class of the Tin Man, and probably also lacked Dorothy's keen table presence. It is difficult to stay focused on the bridge when your main aim at the table is to be irritable, unpleasant, or downright evil! While the Lion was a sound, if rather unimaginative and conservative player, all three nasty witches were reckoned to have the edge on him.

So the decision for the Club Handicapping Committee had eventually focused on the actual handicaps in each of the teams, Glinda and the Scarecrow. There was no doubting that Glinda had her deficiencies. Indeed, kibitzing her as declarer for even just one hand usually revealed many shortcomings. However, no discussion was needed to agree that she could not possibly be considered to counterbalance the Scarecrow. And so it was solely because Dorothy's team were the defending champions that they had been given a slightly higher handicap and began the match 4 IMPs behind.

Auntie Em had come to kibitz against the Wicked Witch. Deciding whom to support wasn't a problem for her. The Lion may have riled her by gloating over the doubled Six Clubs he made in the semifinal, but she knew at heart that she deserved it after her comments on the +1130 the Lion and the Scarecrow donated to her earlier in the match. Not that she would ever let the Lion know that, and in any other circumstances, she would have been happy to see him fail in the final.

However, these were not any other circumstances. The Lion's team was playing the final against the witches. Whatever sins may have been committed by the members of the Lion's team, they paled in significance compared to those of the Wicked Witch. Auntie Em would have supported the devil herself in a match against that woman.

The Club tried to respect cultural diversity, something the witches took advantage of by insisting that they sit in their namesake seats throughout, forcing Dorothy's team to switch after each segment.

"Preposterous," muttered the Tin Man. "They seem to cope when we're playing a Howell movement."

It suited Auntie Em, however. She drew up her chair as close as possible behind the Wicked Witch of the West's seat in the Open Room. She would happily put up with discomfort for the next three hours if she could manage to have a suitable effect on the result.

For the first set of six boards, Dorothy and the Tin Man were to sit East-West against Irritable and Unpleasant. Elegant as ever, Glinda walked past on her way to the Open Room and smiled at them all.

As they opened the door of the Closed Room, the Unpleasant Witch confided to Dorothy, "Not as young as she looks, you know. Got a nice line in anti-aging products — not that she would ever admit it."

This was an early declarer play problem for the Irritable Witch:

```
        ♠ 10 8 4
        ♡ A K 8 4
        ◇ Q 5 4 3
        ♣ Q 3
        ┌──────────┐
        └──────────┘
        ♠ A Q J 7
        ♡ J 7 3
        ◇ A K 10 2
        ♣ 4 2
```

With North-South vulnerable, the bidding had gone:

West	North	East	South
Tin Man	Unpleasant	Dorothy	Irritable
			1NT
4♣	dbl	pass	4♠
all pass			

The Irritable Witch, as South, had a problem after her partner's double. At any other vulnerability, she would have passed, seeking the penalty. She might also have passed had the Scarecrow been at the helm. However, with the Tin Man as declarer, while the penalty would most likely be 500, it could well be less. It looked too dangerous not to go for the vulnerable game.

The Tin Man began with the top clubs, Dorothy playing the nine followed by the seven. He then switched to the ◇8. The Irritable Witch considered running this to hand, but she wanted to be in dummy as soon as possible to finesse trumps, and if Dorothy, in the East seat, held four diamonds to the jack, then they could be picked up later. Irritable called for the queen and was surprised when Dorothy contributed the jack.

It was clear that the Tin Man held seven clubs and it now looked as if he also held four diamonds. With eleven of his cards in the minors, the chances of bringing in the majors for one loser did not look good for declarer. The Irritable Witch called for the ♠10, covered by Dorothy's king. She won with the ace, the Tin Man contributing the five. Her next move was to cash the ♠Q, unblocking the eight from dummy as the Tin Man discarded a club. She crossed to the ♡A, all following, and finessed the ♠7. The full layout was now an open book:

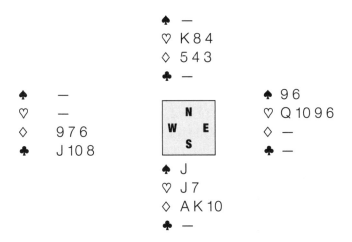

	♠ —	
	♡ K 8 4	
	◇ 5 4 3	
	♣ —	
♠ —		♠ 9 6
♡ —		♡ Q 10 9 6
◇ 9 7 6		◇ —
♣ J 10 8		♣ —
	♠ J	
	♡ J 7	
	◇ A K 10	
	♣ —	

The Irritable Witch of the South played her last trump, then switched to diamonds. Dorothy discarded hearts on the ace and king in the hope that her partner had the ◇10, but when declarer produced it she ruffed in and tried the ♡10. Declarer hopped in with the jack and scored the king as her tenth trick.

The full hand had been:

Dealer South. N/S vul.

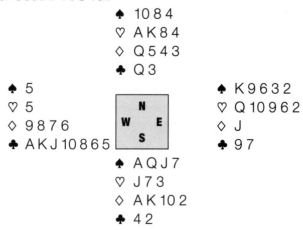

```
                    ♠ 10 8 4
                    ♥ A K 8 4
                    ♦ Q 5 4 3
                    ♣ Q 3
     ♠ 5                          ♠ K 9 6 3 2
     ♥ 5              N           ♥ Q 10 9 6 2
     ♦ 9 8 7 6    W     E         ♦ J
     ♣ A K J 10 8 6 5   S         ♣ 9 7
                    ♠ A Q J 7
                    ♥ J 7 3
                    ♦ A K 10 2
                    ♣ 4 2
```

The Unpleasant Witch of the North sniffed noisily, her pleasure at the good score tempered by her being unable to find any criticism of her partner.

"Well, at least you made it," she grumbled. "I suppose we could only have taken 500 defending Four Clubs doubled."

In the other room, Glinda was sitting East against the Scarecrow and the Lion. The latter was finding it hard to concentrate in the presence of Glinda's cascading hair, currently strawberry blonde, and beautiful blue eyes. The Scarecrow always found it hard to concentrate, and was caught between terror of the Wicked Witch of the West and the reassurance of having a kindly opponent at the table.

The Scarecrow opened One Notrump and the Wicked Witch of the West decided to lie low with her seven-card club suit. After a routine Stayman auction, the Scarecrow found himself in Three Notrump. The Wicked Witch led the ♣A and the Lion tabled his hand.

"Slightly worried about clubs," he said. "Hope the queen helps."

"Not much," cackled the Wicked Witch when everyone followed to the second round. Through careful discarding, the Scarecrow was capable of holding on to his six top tricks, so the contract went three down.

As he sat sadly contemplating his losers, Glinda squeezed his hand and said, "Don't worry, there was nothing you could do."

True as that was, he sat tensely later at the scoring up as the 14 IMP loss came out. The Scarecrow was astonished when the Tin Man silently moved on to the next board, without even discussing the merits of his Four Club overcall.

After the first quarter, the witches had extended their lead to 20 IMPs. For the second quarter, the Tin Man and Dorothy made their way through to the Open Room to sit North-South against Glinda and the Wicked Witch of the West. Auntie Em remained where she had sat forlornly for the first session. She pulled her chair even closer to the Witch's chair. Perhaps the Tin Man and Dorothy would put her under more pressure than the Lion and the Scarecrow had managed to produce, and then perhaps her discomfort, aided by a few well-timed coughs, might produce results.

Much to the delight of Auntie Em, the set began with a number of positive positions for the Tin Man and Dorothy. She couldn't be sure how much of this was due to Glinda's incompetence or to the Wicked Witch's discomfort. She was proud, however, of the easy slam that had been missed; she would definitely have bid on with the Witch's hand, but the Wicked Witch had seemed more interested in shifting her seat than in bidding the hand. And then there was the hand where Glinda went five down in Three Notrump, non-vulnerable and sadly undoubled, when Four Spades was an easy make. A loud clearing of her throat at just the right moment in the auction must have had some effect.

Then the Tin Man found himself declaring Three Notrump after an unopposed auction:

♠ K 9 8 7 5
♡ K 9 4 2
♢ A Q 8
♣ 10

♠ 10 2
♡ A Q 8
♢ K 7 4 3
♣ K 8 5 2

West	North	East	South
Wicked	*Dorothy*	*Glinda*	*Tin Man*
	1♠	pass	2♣
pass	2♡	pass	3NT
all pass			

The ♢6 was led and the Tin Man looked for the best line in what may not have been the best of games, but was undoubtedly the best game available. Perhaps Two Notrump from him would have been a better bid. Knowing that Glinda was half the defensive team had influenced his thinking. However, he had played a part in the 14 IMP swing in the first session, and this made it all the more important that he bring this contract in.

If both red suits broke, he would have eight tricks and could hope for a ninth from one of the black kings. If only one red suit broke, then he would probably need both aces to be correctly placed. Playing on spades might give him the tricks he needed, but the defense was sure to find clubs and set up enough tricks to defeat him.

Keeping his communications fluid, the Tin Man won the first trick with the ♢A. The fall of the jack on his right gave him a strong indication that the suit was 4-2. If that was the case, was there anything better than playing for hearts being 3-3, and both black kings to score? Yes — if West held the ♠A, then it might be possible to arrange an endplay and force her to play the clubs to him.

Returning to his hand with the ♡Q, leaving doubt in the mind of the Wicked Witch about the position of the ♡A, he led the ♠10. When West played low, he went up with the king, which scored. Just in case East had started with queen to three, he played the ♠7 back towards his hand to give the defense the maximum chance to go wrong. But it was irrelevant, as the Wicked Witch of the West won the ace.

She played back a low heart, won by the ace in declarer's hand, Glinda contributing the ten. Everything was now set for the endplay. The Tin Man ran off the two top diamonds and all his hearts, ending in dummy. At this point, he had lost only one trick. West was known to have the master diamond, but what was her spade holding? If she had started with ♠ AQJ3, surely she would have risen with the ace on the first round. Confidently, the Tin Man exited with a spade.

In fact, these were the remaining cards:

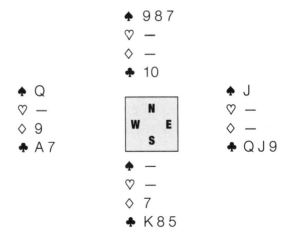

Winning this trick left the Wicked Witch on play and allowed the Tin Man to score his ninth trick at the end with the ♣K. The full hand had been:

```
              ♠ K 9 8 7 5
              ♡ K 9 4 2
              ♢ A Q 8
              ♣ 10
♠ A Q 3                        ♠ J 6 4
♡ 7 6 5        ┌─────────┐     ♡ J 10 3
♢ 9 6 5 2      │   N     │     ♢ J 10
♣ A 7 4        │ W    E  │     ♣ Q J 9 6 3
               │   S     │
               └─────────┘
              ♠ 10 2
              ♡ A Q 8
              ♢ K 7 4 3
              ♣ K 8 5 2
```

The Tin Man turned to Glinda in the East seat. "Nice ending, if I may say so myself," he said. "Even if you had held both remaining spades and the ace of clubs, I would still be making the contract, while if you had the spades and your partner held the ace of clubs, there was no chance anyway."

Glinda smiled at him uncomprehendingly. The Tin Man had obviously done something clever and clearly needed praise. "Yes, that was a beautiful play. I must study it later."

Her partner, the Wicked Witch of the West, grunted. "Flat board, I would think. Even that cretin, the Irritable Witch of the South, should be able to spot a baby endplay like that."

In the other room, the Scarecrow had reached the table in a happy daze after Glinda's kindness, but he was soon brought back to reality by the malevolent presence of Irritable and Unpleasant. The first few hands did not go well for them, particularly in the bidding department, and he was not unhappy when a hand came along on which he had nothing to do but pass. With the Lion also silent throughout, the witches bid unopposed to Three Notrump with the same auction that the Tin Man and Dorothy had produced.

Reading the auction beautifully, the Scarecrow identified diamonds as the unbid suit and fished out the six.

The Irritable Witch wasn't enthused by the sight of dummy and decided it was time for preemptive action, before her own Three Notrump bid was questioned.

"Call that an opening bid with these gappy suits?"

The Unpleasant Witch of the North snorted. "Of course I do. Everyone would. If this goes down, it won't be due to my bidding."

Declarer tried to form a plan. To pass the time of day, she decided to ask a few questions. It was always a good tactic to ask questions. An incorrect or partial answer could create extra chances of a win at the Appeal Committee.

"What are your leads?" she asked the Lion.

"Top of a doubleton, fourth from an honor, and second from poor suits," the Lion replied.

"And do you count the ten as an honor?" she went on, mostly trying to buy time. The Lion grunted in the affirmative. This didn't really aid her understanding: diamonds could be 3-3 or 4-2 either way, and no finesse position was likely to emerge.

Eventually, she alighted on the same line as the Tin Man: she came to hand with a heart and led out the ♠10. At this point, the play at the two tables diverged with the Scarecrow putting in the queen. Hoping that this was from ace-queen doubleton, declarer put up the king and was pleased when it scored. Next, she cashed the hearts, pitching a club from hand, then tried the top diamonds. When they proved to be 4-2, she fell back on her second chance, exiting with the last diamond to West. At this stage they were down to:

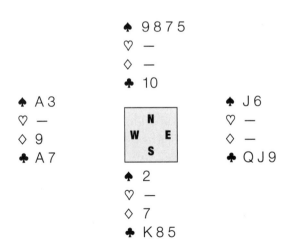

```
              ♠ 9 8 7 5
              ♡ —
              ◇ —
              ♣ 10
  ♠ A 3                        ♠ J 6
  ♡ —          N              ♡ —
  ◇ 9       W     E           ◇ —
  ♣ A 7        S              ♣ Q J 9
              ♠ 2
              ♡ —
              ◇ 7
              ♣ K 8 5
```

This was a similar position to that reached by the Tin Man but with the crucial difference that after winning the diamond, the Scarecrow was able to play ace and another spade to the Lion's jack. The ♣Q through declarer's king finished her off.

"I'm wondering if it would be worthwhile asking what led you to unblock the queen of spades," whined the Irritable Witch of the South.

"Oh no, I wasn't unblocking. I was covering an honor with an honor. Your question about leads had reminded me that we treat the ten as an honor, you see."

"Very well done, partner," interjected the Unpleasant Witch of the North. "It seems that if you hadn't asked that fatuous question, you might have made the contract. And, no, it wasn't worth asking about the unblock — that was another fatuous question."

The set had not gone terribly well for the Scarecrow and the Lion. As they went through to their teammates, they could tell that the Tin Man was eager to score up, which only made them feel worse.

"Minus 680," he called out before they had even finished sitting down. "We preempted them out of slam."

"Plus 230, lose 10 IMPs," said the Lion, not mentioning that his opponents had passed throughout.

"Oh, well, on the next board, we were plus 250, very good defense, if I may say so," the Tin Man continued.

"Minus 300, lose 2 IMPs," said the Lion.

"Were you doubled?"

"No."

After two more disappointing hands, they reached the Three Notrump contract the Tin Man had made. He called out plus 400, and was met by plus 50 and gain of 10 IMPs. A 500 penalty on a partscore hand after a tiger double by Dorothy had brought in another swing, and her team found that they had managed to recoup 8 IMPs to reduce the deficit to 12.

They went to the line for coffee and found themselves standing behind the witches. The Tin Man was in the lead.

"Interesting Three Notrump," he said to the Irritable Witch of the South.

"Yes, but you can't make it," she scowled back.

"On a diamond lead, which we both received, you can always make it, as it happens."

"Harrumph. Always goes down." The Irritable Witch turned her back on him.

"Ah, yes, not an obvious endplay on West, I'll grant you," said the Tin Man, making only a slight effort not to sound too smug.

Taking the bait, the Irritable Witch turned to face him. "Oh, the endplay was obvious enough. I just didn't get the helpful defense that you did. It can never make."

"I'd like to see you beat it," retorted the Tin Man.

"Okay, if I can beat it, you buy my coffees. If you make it, I'll buy yours."

The Tin Man agreed and listened unconcernedly to the Irritable Witch's account of the play at her table

"Duck the queen of spades," he said. "You want West on lead, not East. There's no rush to take the spade. Taking the king was your mistake. Win the diamond continuation, come back to hand with another heart, and lead your last spade. Then his goose is completely cooked. If he ducks, you will endplay him. If he wins, then spades are good."

"What diamond continuation?" snapped the Irritable Witch. "I am switching to a club to partner's jack. If you win it, then I will win the ace of spades next time and we cash out. If you duck, then we play clubs through you."

The Tin Man was shocked by his oversight. "Are you saying that the Scarecrow would have found a club switch?"

"I don't recall him being part of the bet. I'm switching to a club, the contract is going down, and you are buying my extra-large coffee. I expect you thought it was your good play that won your team the swing when it was actually the Scarecrow's defense. Perhaps you should buy his coffee too."

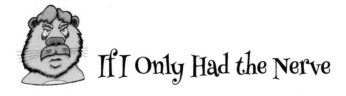# If I Only Had the Nerve

The Lion stomped unhappily into the other room to play the last set of six boards in the final of the club's Handicap Cup. They had started the match with a handicap of 4 IMPs against the witches, but after the first set, the deficit had been increased to 20 IMPs. Wins by 8 IMPs in each of the next two sets brought them back to where they had started, with just the final set of six boards to go.

Comparing scores with the Tin Man wasn't the Lion's — or for that matter anyone else's — idea of fun. Indeed, he sometimes felt that surgery without anesthetic might be less of an ordeal. The scoring up of the third set had been a particularly unpleasant experience. The Tin Man seemed to think that he and Dorothy had a good card and was far from satisfied with the actual win by 8 IMPs.

The Wicked Witch of the West had made a Three Notrump with six top losers, but how had he been supposed to find a lead from ♠A2 when he had another suit of QJ109? One of the Scarecrow's spades had looked very club-like during the auction so he hadn't opened the routine weak two in spades as the Irritable Witch of the South had done at the other table.

Then, admittedly, there was the pushy Four Spades their opposition had made despite the serious handicap of having Glinda at the helm. Dorothy, at the other table, had had to rely on a double squeeze to make her Three Spades partscore. The Scarecrow had just read an article in which the lead of small from a doubleton honor had worked wonders. He had been concentrating and listening carefully to the auction. It sounded just like the one in the book, and he had a doubleton king. He had felt it was unlucky that this wasn't the moment for it. Even Glinda, despite apparently trying hard to fail, couldn't quite manage it after that lead.

But they had still won the set by 8 IMPs, and that was due in no small measure to them defeating Glinda's vulnerable One Notrump by two tricks. She had seven top tricks, but having been chastised for turning down risk-free finesses earlier in the match, she'd shown the merit of her earlier caution, taking two finesses that were wrong in more ways than one. The Tin Man had insisted on focusing on these other hands and hadn't wanted to hear how this defense had gone.

He certainly had made it abundantly clear that in his opinion, the match should have been wrapped up by now, and the blame for the fact that it wasn't certainly lay with his teammates.

"I'll show him," the Lion muttered. "I'll show that rusty tin can. The cheek of him... so easy after the hand — anyone can do that. Just one chance, that's all I need."

Dorothy was only too well aware of the effect her partner was having on her teammates, but it was too late to do anything. She took the North seat and extracted her hand from the first board. She found herself looking at a 1=5=6=1 9-count and decided to open it. In order to get both her suits into the auction, she started proceedings with a bid of One Heart.

This was the full hand:

Dealer North. N/S vul.

```
                    ♠ 8
                    ♡ K J 8 6 2
                    ◇ A J 9 6 5 4
                    ♣ 10
  ♠ 10 7 5                           ♠ A J 6 3 2
  ♡ Q 10 7 4        ┌─────────┐      ♡ 9 3
  ◇ K 3 2           │    N    │      ◇ 10 8 7
  ♣ J 6 2           │ W     E │      ♣ A 9 5
                    │    S    │
                    └─────────┘
                    ♠ K Q 9 4
                    ♡ A 5
                    ◇ Q
                    ♣ K Q 8 7 4 3
```

West	North	East	South
Wicked	*Dorothy*	*Glinda*	*Tin Man*
	1♡	1♠	2♣
pass	2◇	pass	3NT
all pass			

Her partner's Three Notrump was the last thing she wanted
to hear. Her hand was clearly worth an opening bid if it found
a fit with partner. It looked distinctly less attractive when
partner didn't like either suit. She knew that the Tin Man was
going to be disappointed with dummy, but from experience she
also knew that it would do no good to insist on one of her suits.
She would just have to take her medicine in the post-mortem
if the contract failed.

The Wicked Witch of the West pulled out the ♠5, leading
her partner's suit. Glinda won the trick with the ace, and returned the ♠3 to declarer's king with dummy discarding a diamond.

The Tin Man stared disconsolately at the dummy in front
of him. He had limited communication between the hands and
a choice of three suits to tackle, each with only a seven-card
fit. None of them looked appetizing. The only consolation was
that there was no obvious suit for the defense to tackle.

He started with the ◇Q, which held the trick, and then the ♣K, which Glinda won with the ace. She now played her ♣2. The Tin Man put in the nine, leaving West to win the trick as he discarded a heart from dummy. The Wicked Witch switched to a heart, which the Tin Man won in hand with the ace, leaving this position, having both won and lost three tricks:

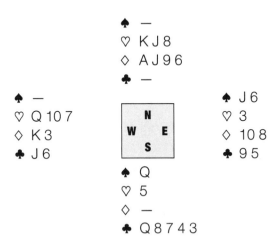

```
                    ♠ —
                    ♡ K J 8
                    ◇ A J 9 6
                    ♣ —
    ♠ —                             ♠ J 6
    ♡ Q 10 7         N              ♡ 3
    ◇ K 3        W       E          ◇ 10 8
    ♣ J 6            S              ♣ 9 5
                    ♠ Q
                    ♡ 5
                    ◇ —
                    ♣ Q 8 7 4 3
```

The Tin Man laid the ♣Q on the table, discarding a diamond from dummy. He now played the ♠Q. This left the Wicked Witch feeling distinctly uncomfortable. She couldn't afford any red card, so discarded her ♣J, relying on her partner holding the ♣9 to stop declarer, the Tin Man, from running the rest of this suit.

The Tin Man had seen the Wicked Witch squirm. He now took the heart finesse by playing the five to the jack, and when this held, he faced his hand with a flourish.

"I shall be cashing the king of hearts, and if the queen falls, I have nine tricks conceding a diamond at the end. If it doesn't, then I shall exit with the eight of hearts, and you," he turned and looked with disdain at the Wicked Witch, "will then have the pleasure of allowing me to take a second diamond finesse."

Glinda looked on uncomprehendingly. "Well done," she said.

The Wicked Witch sniffed and put her cards back in the board. "Nothing to it," she said, sneering at the Tin Man. "Even the Irritable Witch of the South should be capable of that."

"Well played," said Dorothy, ignoring her. "I was aware dummy wasn't ideal."

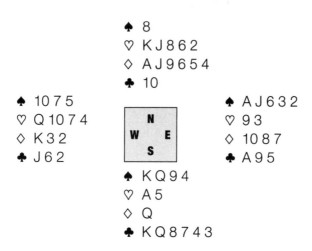

```
              ♠ 8
              ♡ K J 8 6 2
              ◊ A J 9 6 5 4
              ♣ 10
♠ 10 7 5                        ♠ A J 6 3 2
♡ Q 10 7 4         N            ♡ 9 3
◊ K 3 2         W     E         ◊ 10 8 7
♣ J 6 2            S            ♣ A 9 5
              ♠ K Q 9 4
              ♡ A 5
              ◊ Q
              ♣ K Q 8 7 4 3
```

The auction was identical in the other room, and the Lion, sitting West, took the safe course of leading his partner's suit. In at Trick 2 with her ♠K, the Irritable Witch of the South followed almost the same line of play as the Tin Man. The ◊Q held and she followed it up with the ♣Q.

With the match so close, the Scarecrow was trying to give every card played his full attention, not that in his case that amounted to much. Seeing the ♣Q, suddenly he saw how to defeat this contract. Clearly, partner had the ♣K, and if the Lion took it on the next round, the spades could be cleared and he would still have his ♣A as an entry.

When her ♣Q held the trick, the Irritable Witch thought for a moment. She still had spades guarded — the suit the defense was sure to play — and she had the ♡A in hand. As long as clubs were 3-3, she would have time to set up the clubs and be able to enjoy them. A doubleton ace would also help, making her ♣K a winner. She led the ♣8. The Lion was suspicious. Could declarer have the 9-8? He rose with the jack and returned the ♠10, declarer winning with the queen. The players were now down to:

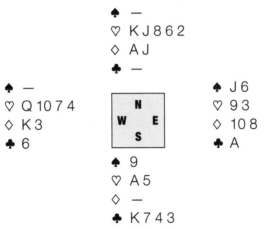

```
                    ♠ —
                    ♡ K J 8 6 2
                    ◇ A J
                    ♣ —
    ♠ —                              ♠ J 6
    ♡ Q 10 7 4          N            ♡ 9 3
    ◇ K 3          W        E        ◇ 10 8
    ♣ 6                 S            ♣ A
                    ♠ 9
                    ♡ A 5
                    ◇ —
                    ♣ K 7 4 3
```

The Irritable Witch surveyed the hand for a few minutes. She had taken two spade tricks, the ♣Q, and the ◇Q — four tricks in total. She still had the ◇A and the two top hearts, bringing the total to seven. Continuing clubs did not seem like a good plan, as the Scarecrow would have the ace for his overcall and his last remaining spades were now good. She turned her mind to piecing together the Lion's West hand. He seemed to have started with three spades, and from his hesitation on the previous trick, it looked like he had three clubs. It seemed entirely possible that he had three hearts to the queen, in which case dummy's heart suit would provide her eighth and ninth tricks.

She played the ♡A, and then overcame the first hurdle when the finesse of the ♡J won. However, the heart suit failed to break, and she drifted one down.

Not waiting for the play to finish, the Unpleasant Witch of the North leaned across the table. "I'm glad you took so long to think about the endgame, partner," she said in a clearly menacing tone, "but wouldn't it have been a better idea to do so one trick earlier? After giving West a trick with his jack of clubs, all you have to do is give him another one with his ten of spades! Nothing he can lead can do you any harm, and you still have the spades stopped. What is he supposed to lead next?" She cackled.

"You might even have given it some thought after your queen of clubs won," she continued, lapping up her partner's obvious discomfort. "Your right-hand opponent hesitated long enough on the first club trick to tell the world and his uncle that he had the ace. Why not play the king of clubs next to ensure the danger hand wins that trick rather than a later one?" She sat back in her seat smugly. "And you can explain that hand to Wicked."

For someone who had just seen a probable loss of 12 IMPs, the Unpleasant Witch of the North looked surprisingly happy. The thought of the confrontation later between her partner and the Wicked Witch of the West, assisted by some appropriate stirring from her good self made her grin.

The Irritable Witch of the South remained tight-lipped. She knew she was on weak ground, but consoled herself with the thought that the next time her partner made a mistake, she wouldn't hold back. It might almost be worth letting her play a few hands just to get some ammunition!

When the last board was placed on the table, the Lion knew the match was very close. Every IMP was likely to count. With both sides vulnerable, he picked up:

♠ K J   ♡ A J 9   ◇ K Q J 10 7   ♣ 10 9 4

After two passes, the Irritable Witch of the South opened One Heart. Summoning up all his courage, the Lion overcalled One Notrump, and tried, with only limited success, to remain calm when the Unpleasant Witch of the North doubled. The Scarecrow and South both passed and the Lion removed himself to Two Diamonds with the best attempt at nonchalance that he could muster. North now bid Three Clubs, much to the Lion's relief, and South paused for thought. She tried Three Diamonds, and after her partner's Three Spades, she bid Three Notrump, which brought the auction to an end.

West	North	East	South
Lion	Unpleasant	Scarecrow	Irritable
	pass	pass	1♡
1NT	dbl	pass	pass
2◊	3♣	pass	3◊
pass	3♠	pass	3NT
all pass			

The Lion felt on solid, unimpeachable ground in leading the king of diamonds, after which he could see:

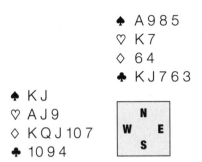

```
              ♠ A 9 8 5
              ♡ K 7
              ◊ 6 4
              ♣ K J 7 6 3
  ♠ K J
  ♡ A J 9        N
  ◊ K Q J 10 7  W   E
  ♣ 10 9 4        S
```

Declarer took some time to duck Trick 1, giving the Lion time to consider the defense. He could see that declarer had at most five club tricks, one diamond, and a spade on top. Once the ◊A was dislodged, then he would have five tricks in his hand, so the contract would be one down. If declarer wasn't careful, then in trying to set up an eighth or ninth trick, a sixth trick might appear for the defenders. That would be a score to show the Tin Man, and an extra vulnerable undertrick might be critical.

With the Scarecrow showing an even number, South won the second diamond and led a heart towards the dummy. The Lion ducked smoothly, setting up a tenace over declarer's queen when the king scored. However, instead of continuing hearts, declarer switched to clubs. She won the ace and queen in hand and returned to dummy with a third one. Declarer and the Lion discarded hearts on the fourth club, leaving this position:

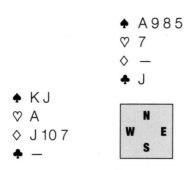

                    ♠ A 9 8 5
                    ♡ 7
                    ◇ —
                    ♣ J

    ♠ K J
    ♡ A   ┌─────────┐
    ◇ J 10 7   │   N   │
    ♣ —   │ W   E │
                         │   S   │
                         └─────────┘

On the fifth club, declarer threw a spade, and the Lion found
himself with an impossible problem. His head was pounding.
Why had he not followed his instincts and simply taken his
five tricks when he had the chance? A spade was out of the
question, as was the ♡A, so he had to discard one of his diamond
winners. Declarer's next move was to put him in with the ♡A.
He cashed his two diamonds, but then he had to broach the
spade suit, giving declarer her ninth trick with the queen.
This was the full hand:

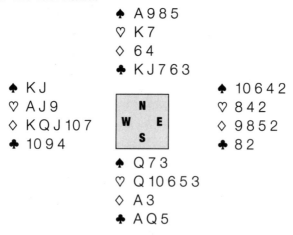

                    ♠ A 9 8 5
                    ♡ K 7
                    ◇ 6 4
                    ♣ K J 7 6 3
    ♠ K J   ♠ 10 6 4 2
    ♡ A J 9   ┌─────────┐   ♡ 8 4 2
    ◇ K Q J 10 7   │   N   │   ◇ 9 8 5 2
    ♣ 10 9 4   W│   E │   ♣ 8 2
                        │   S   │
                        └─────────┘
                    ♠ Q 7 3
                    ♡ Q 10 6 5 3
                    ◇ A 3
                    ♣ A Q 5

The other table was still in play. The Lion pretended to turn
on his mobile phone. "I've just got an urgent text message," he
told the Scarecrow, putting his coat on. "You can let me know
the result later."

    "But they are just finishing," called the Scarecrow to his
partner's hastily retreating back.

    "Sorry, must hurry!" called the Lion as the door shut.

9

If Ever a Wiz There Was...

In the aftermath of the last board loss to the Witches in the final of the Handicap Cup, the Lion absented himself from all bridge commitments for the following week. It seemed that he had a friend who was struggling with an undefined problem and required someone to stand by him in an incredibly brave way.

This left the Scarecrow at something of a loose end. He had a high capacity for playing bridge, as he put much less mental effort into it than most people. He fondly remembered the time that the Tin Man had remarked that he was every bit as sharp at the end of a long match as he was at the start. With the Lion suddenly unavailable for a week, he was left without a partner for three nights. He approached Dorothy, who agreed to play with him on Monday night. For the sake of her sanity, she felt that she could not risk any more than that. For Wednesday night, she fixed him up with her Uncle Henry, but only after accepting the latter's condition that she play with Uncle Henry on Friday. The Wednesday game did not go well. For some reason the Scarecrow and Uncle Henry did not gel: Henry's inflexible approach jarred with the Scarecrow's unintentional flair. It was a disaster that left both men shaken and club members wondering if they had ever seen a worse score than 28 percent.

It looked as if the Scarecrow would be without a game on Friday. More out of habit than anything else, he turned up at the club with a view to watching some of the better players. About fifteen minutes before the start of play, he was sitting at the bar sipping lemonade when a distinguished-looking stranger walked through the door. He approached the barman, gave him a pleasant smile, and asked if he could speak to someone in charge. As the barman went to find the tournament director, the Scarecrow stepped in.

"Hello. I'm not in charge in any sense, but I wonder if I could be of any help?"

"That's very kind of you," said the stranger, turning his smile onto the Scarecrow and offering him his hand. "I know that this is ridiculously short notice, but I am in town on business for a couple of days and stopped by in the hope of getting a game."

"What tremendous luck! It so happens that I'm without a partner myself tonight and I would be very happy to play with you. By the way, I couldn't help noticing your accent. Would I be right in assuming that you are from Norway?"

The stranger's smile widened. "Close enough. Australia."

The Scarecrow visibly brightened. "Wonderful. I do love Ron Klinger's books. I believe I have read them all, and I'm fairly sure I've read some of them twice. I think you'll find the standard here a bit mixed but the players are friendly. I'm sure you'll always get a warm welcome at the table with me as your partner." They discussed their system earnestly for the next few minutes, and then launched into the evening's session.

The Australian proved himself to be quite handy with the cards and rescued the Scarecrow from a few misbids and misdefenses. At half-time, the stranger felt it wise to try and clear up some misunderstandings that the Scarecrow had picked up from his reading.

"Thank you so much," said the Scarecrow afterwards. "I can see that I totally misunderstood Mr. Klinger's book on Losing Trick Count. I thought it was like point count and that the more you had, the better it was."

"Next time I see him, I'll suggest he makes that a bit clearer," the Australian said, smiling.

The second half went well for the new pair, with good scores outweighing disasters. Going into the last round, it was clear that they were nicely placed.

"I don't want to make you nervous," the Scarecrow whispered to his partner, "but I think that two good boards would give us about 60 percent!" Their opponents were another irregular partnership: Dorothy and Uncle Henry approached their table and sat down to play.

"Welcome to the club," said Dorothy. "I hope you are enjoying your game."

"Very much so," said the Australian. "I have been very lucky to get a game at such short notice, and with such a pleasant partner. I'll have lots to tell the people back home."

"I bet you will," muttered Uncle Henry under his breath.

This was the first of the two hands in the round.

Dealer South. Neither vul.

```
                ♠ 10 5 2
                ♡ 7 4
                ◊ A K 6 5
                ♣ Q J 10 8
♠ —                              ♠ Q J 9 4 3
♡ K J 10 8 2      N              ♡ A
◊ Q J 10 8 2   W     E           ◊ 9 4 3
♣ 9 4 2          S               ♣ 7 6 5 3
                ♠ A K 8 7 6
                ♡ Q 9 6 5 3
                ◊ 7
                ♣ A K
```

South, the Australian, opened One Spade and Uncle Henry overcalled Two Spades, showing hearts and a minor. His natural instincts were to play this cuebid as showing a powerhouse, but in a nod to the 1960s, he had agreed to update to Michaels. The Scarecrow raised to Three Spades and Dorothy passed. Though not without some concerns about his hearts, the Australian bid Four Spades and, after two passes, Dorothy doubled.

Uncle Henry led the ◊Q and the Australian quickly assessed the dummy. With clubs blocked, trumps breaking badly, and a pile of heart losers, prospects did not look good. He ducked the opening lead and Uncle Henry continued with the ◊J. Years of practice enabled Dorothy to keep a straight face. It was such a wooden play, but she still felt confident that the contract was going down.

Declarer won this trick, casually discarding the ♣K, then played the other top diamond to discard his remaining top club. Three rounds of clubs now allowed three hearts to be discarded. The Australian noted with double pleasure the fall of the ♣9. It meant both that his eight was a master and that West, having started with three clubs, clearly had started with a 0=5=5=3 shape. He could now safely play the fourth club from dummy and pitch another heart. Next came a spade from the dummy, and he finessed the six. With five tricks to go, this was the position, declarer having lost only the opening trick:

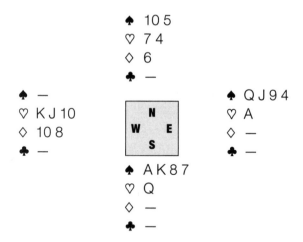

Declarer led the ♡Q from his hand. Uncle Henry put up the king, but Dorothy had to win the ace. Dorothy stopped to think. A low trump would obviously be fatal because declarer would run it to dummy's ten. She tried the ♠Q. The Australian won that and played another spade to dummy's ten and Dorothy's jack. For the second time in three tricks, she was endplayed, declarer having ♠K8 over her ♠94.

"Well played," she said, conceding the last two.

The Scarecrow entered the score into the Bridgemate. "Gosh, partner, you seem to be the only person to have made Four Spades, despite that slip when you played low on the opening lead." He examined his partner's hand uncomprehendingly.

The stranger smiled. "Yes, I was probably the only declarer to lose a diamond trick. Sorry about that."

"Did you have to double?" Uncle Henry asked Dorothy. "All you did was tip him off to the bad break."

This was a real test for Dorothy. She had a glazed expression for a second, then said, "You could be right. Perhaps we should ask Auntie Em about the hand when I take you home."

The Scarecrow started to tingle with excitement as he placed the second and final board on the table. He had never scored as high as 60 percent before. Now one decent board was all that stood between him and that achievement. Who knew, they might even have a chance of winning!

Uncle Henry passed, and after less than a minute, the Scarecrow realized it was his bid, holding:

♠AK876 ♡Q9653 ◇7 ♣AK

Vulnerable against not, he opened One Spade. The Australian responded Three Hearts. The Scarecrow's heart jumped. Not only would he get his best-ever score, but he would also round it all off with a bang! Surely there was a slam in this — perhaps even a grand slam!

Seeing no point in hanging back, he jumped to four notrump. His partner had declined to play anything other than basic Blackwood, which made his Five Spades reply extremely unexpected. Checking his addition, the Scarecrow concluded that they had five aces between them. He had heard people talking about fancy keycard systems where the queen of trumps was an extra ace — or was it the jack? His own experience of trying to master such methods had been added to the bulging file of disasters best forgotten about. Surely his partner would remember that they weren't playing anything like that. He pressed on with Five Notrump, to which his partner responded Six Spades. Five aces and five kings? The Scarecrow's head was spinning, but nonetheless, too many aces was surely better than too few. He bid Seven Hearts and when Uncle Henry doubled, he redoubled.

Uncle Henry led the ♠10 and the Scarecrow laid dummy down. He had scarcely got the trumps on the table when the other three players at the table started to protest.

"What's going on here?" cried Dorothy. "You've got some of my cards!"

"And mine," added Uncle Henry.

"You've got my entire hand," said the Australian, "from the last board."

Sure enough, the North cards were still untouched on the board. Trembling with shame and fear, the Scarecrow extracted his real hand. This was the actual full deal:

Dealer West. N/S vul.

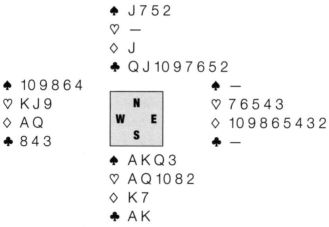

```
                    ♠ J 7 5 2
                    ♡ —
                    ◇ J
                    ♣ Q J 10 9 7 6 5 2
  ♠ 10 9 8 6 4                        ♠ —
  ♡ K J 9             N               ♡ 7 6 5 4 3
  ◇ A Q          W        E           ◇ 10 9 8 6 5 4 3 2
  ♣ 8 4 3             S               ♣ —
                    ♠ A K Q 3
                    ♡ A Q 10 8 2
                    ◇ K 7
                    ♣ A K
```

The spade was ruffed and a diamond returned to the queen. The play continued: second spade ruff; diamond to the ace; third spade ruff; diamond ruffed with the queen and overruffed; fourth spade ruff; diamond ruffed with the ten and overruffed; club ruff. Dorothy now played a fifth diamond. Declarer put in the ♡8, but Henry was able to overruff with his last trump.

The Australian tabled his remaining three cards; the ♡A2 and the ♣A. "As I've managed to pull all the trumps, I think the rest are mine," he said quietly.

"There," said Uncle Henry, with feeling. "That is what a sound double looks like."

The stranger took the Bridgemate and filled it in for the stunned Scarecrow: -5800. "Cheer up, mate," the Australian said. "Think of it as an average round. That's the magic of matchpoints."

Five minutes later, a shaking Scarecrow returned from the toilets. One table was still in play, and as he waited for the results, he looked for his partner. The Australian was nowhere to be seen. He sat down beside Dorothy.

"Don't worry about that last hand," she said sympathetically. "It's the sort of thing that could happen to anyone. How were you doing, apart from that?"

"That's the horror of it," replied the Scarecrow. "I think we might have reached 60 percent. I don't often do that well."

It took a tremendous effort of will power for Dorothy to suppress a smile. The Scarecrow managed over 50 percent about twice in a season, and 55 percent was unheard of.

The director came into the bar carrying the printed page with the results. "We have a tie for third place at 56.3 percent, but clearly ahead in second place with 60.4 percent are Dorothy and Uncle Henry. In first place — " The director paused. "I'll announce the results, but I think we'll hold off giving out prize money tonight until we've checked the scoring. In first place with a score of 68.2 percent are the Scarecrow and his partner, whose name we don't seem to have."

The whole room gasped as one. All eyes turned towards the Scarecrow, who was sitting with his mouth wide open, his hands grasping the chair, a look of total wonderment on his face.

"Well done," said Dorothy. "It was obviously even... even better than you thought. You must have played very well, indeed." Dorothy just managed to finish her sentence before bursting into a coughing fit.

"Yes," said the Scarecrow, "my partner wasn't bad. He made a few silly errors, but then which of us doesn't?"

10

Bridge Over Troubled Waters

In the month following the final of the club Handicap Cup, the Lion had managed to avoid the Tin Man. Indeed, for the first week, he had managed to avoid everybody. He left his house, where the curtains were kept firmly drawn, only to buy basic essentials like milk and bread. Even then, he wore his longest coat with the collar turned up and a hat pulled firmly down.

By the fifth day, he plucked up his courage and actually answered his phone. It was the Scarecrow, wondering if he was well and trying to fix up a few sessions of bridge.

"It's my hay fever," lied the Lion. "It gets so bad at this time of year."

The Scarecrow was not so easily fobbed off. The last board of the Handicap Cup was like so many others to him: what was one extra bad board? Indeed, he hadn't even realized that Three Notrump could and should have been trivially defeated, and that the Lion's failure to do so had cost their team the event. Nor had he understood why the Lion hadn't waited for the comparison. As for the Tin Man's bad temper the following week, that was something he considered part of the normal tapestry of life.

"Oh well, I'll try to come on Tuesday evening for the match-point session." The Lion knew this session was always run as a Mitchell movement with players taking a seat as they came in, then tossing a coin for direction. He reckoned he could find two of his Munchkin fans and sit with them while keeping an eye on the Tin Man's table. The Tin Man liked to get coin-tossing out of the way as soon as possible. If the Tin Man ended up moving, he could graciously concede the sitting seats to his grateful opponents. If the Tin Man ended up sitting North-South, he would have to develop a sore leg!

The Lion had long since explained to the Scarecrow that the choice of starting table was an element of the game best left to his more tactically astute partner. The Scarecrow could be relied upon to relax in the lounge until the Lion had made his nuanced decision.

For the first two weeks, this had worked perfectly. The Lion arrived as late as possible, checked from the hallway that the Tin Man had taken a seat at a table, and then saw the Tin Man and Dorothy move into the East and West seats, respectively.

"He always was a useless tosser," the Lion purred inaudibly under his breath as he edged into the room. He made for one of the tables at the opposite end of the room.

The tea break presented the remaining difficulty. He had taken to playing the round before the break extremely slowly. This allowed Dorothy and the Tin Man to get their tea and settle down at one of the tables in the social area. The Lion could then sidle up to the counter, engage in an earnest conversation with the young student who usually came in to help serve, and then go off with his tea and cookies to the part of the room farthest from the Tin Man.

This hadn't worked on the third week. The third and last board of the round prior to the tea break was passed out at the Lion's table. With sweat oozing from every pore, he practically ran to the counter to get his tea. The student started up a conversation, knowing the Lion to be extremely chatty, but she was surprised when the moment his tea was poured, he rushed away with his cup to the parking lot.

The Tin Man was totally unaware of any problem. The Unpleasant Witch of the North had taken great delight in telling him exactly how the play of that Three Notrump game had gone. To make sure of maximum effect, she and her partner, the Irritable Witch of the South, had raised the subject at least eight times since then. To say that the Tin Man was displeased would have been a serious understatement. Had he met the Lion soon after the match, he would without question have offered him an assessment of his play. It is not clear that the Lion would ever have returned to the bridge table.

However, the Tin Man, knowing in his own mind that he was the best player in the Club by a good margin, was well aware he had to accept that teammates would never be quite good enough, certainly not up to his level. Such was the curse of having his ability. Thank goodness, he thought, he had the humility to accept this situation.

The Tin Man's bad run of coin-tossing came to an end the following week and the Lion saw him taking possession of his table's North seat. The Lion hurried over to a table with two old ladies who waved him to his seat welcomingly. He smiled benevolently at his opponents.

"Would you ladies care to move this week? I hope you don't mind but I hurt my leg last night rescuing a kitten from a tree."

"Oh dear," said the smaller of the pair, "but you were so kind last week in moving, and we invited you to join us in the hope that you would let us sit again. As I told you last time, Cissie is getting her hip replacement surgery next week and it would mean so much to her, wouldn't it, Cissie?"

"Yes, it would, Ada," said Cissie, clutching her handbag tightly to her waist in a way that somehow combined disapproval of the Lion with a sense of possession of the moral high ground, "though I'm very sorry to hear about your leg. I hadn't realized how brave you were being when I saw you jogging this morning."

"Probably best to keep it moving anyway," the Scarecrow said, smiling as he settled into the East seat. "You don't want it to stiffen up."

The Lion gave an involuntary groan, unintentionally in keeping with his feigned injury, and a few minutes later play began. This was the first hand of the evening.

Dealer North. Neither vul.

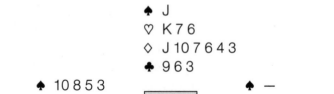

```
                    ♠ J
                    ♡ K 7 6
                    ◊ J 10 7 6 4 3
                    ♣ 9 6 3
   ♠ 10 8 5 3                      ♠ —
   ♡ 10 9 8 4 3 2      N           ♡ Q J
   ◊ A Q          W        E       ◊ K 9 8 5 2
   ♣ 4                  S          ♣ A K Q 8 5 2
                    ♠ A K Q 9 7 6 4 2
                    ♡ A 5
                    ◊ —
                    ♣ J 10 7
```

Ada, sitting North, passed, the Scarecrow opened One Club as East and Cissie overcalled Four Spades. After two passes, the Scarecrow contemplated further action but decided against it. He wondered if Four Notrump might describe his hand type, but had a feeling that it could show the two unbid suits. In any case, he was rarely comfortable at the five-level or above, especially if he might have to play it.

West	North	East	South
Lion	*Ada*	*Scarecrow*	*Cissie*
	pass	1♣	4♠
all pass			

On lead as West, the Lion took the safe course, as usual, and led his partner's suit, his singleton club. The Scarecrow took his three top clubs. The Lion had to make two discards and tried to use them to direct his partner towards diamonds. To that end, he first threw a discouraging ♡2 and then, noticing the vacant look on the Scarecrow's face, followed it up with a discouraging ♡3. The message got through and at Trick 4 a diamond hit the table. Disappointingly for the Lion, declarer ruffed, entered dummy with the ♠J, ruffed another diamond and drew trumps, making the contract.

"Can we do anything else? Did I get it wrong?" the Scarecrow asked.

"No, no. I had hopes for my ace of diamonds but declarer simply has ten on top. At least we got our three top tricks. Five of a minor might be a good save, but with diamonds 6-0, it looks pretty hairy. I think we judged that pretty well."

Three rounds later, just before the break, the board reached the table where Dorothy and the Tin Man were playing against Auntie Em and Uncle Henry. They had the same auction, with Dorothy, as South, becoming declarer. Auntie Em led her club to Uncle Henry's queen. Like the Lion, Auntie Em saw the possibility of scoring a fourth defensive trick in diamonds; unlike him, she realized that contract could be beaten even if declarer was void. On the second club winner, she pitched the ◊Q, and then on the third, she discarded the ace. Henry was awake to the situation and played a diamond at Trick 4. If declarer had followed suit then a ruff would have been the setting trick. As it was, Auntie Em had a guaranteed trump promotion. If Dorothy ruffed low, Em could overruff, and when in fact Dorothy ruffed high, then her ten became a sure trick.

A trump to the jack at the next trick revealed the situation to declarer, who shrugged disappointedly. She tabled her hand. "Good defense, one off."

'Yes, well done, rosebud," said Uncle Henry, well aware that Auntie Em liked her good plays to be appreciated.

The Tin Man snorted. "Sensible defense. Should be a flat board but not in this club."

The Lion, aware that he was destined to play the Tin Man in the second half, spent the mid-session break prowling in the parking lot to the rear. Coffee in hand, Dorothy followed him out. After some awkward pleasantries she said, "You will be playing us in two rounds time. This bad feeling between you and the Tin Man has to stop. We are still teammates, aren't we? More importantly, I hope we are all still friends."

"He just drives me crazy with his smartass comments, trying to make everyone else look dumb."

"Yes, I know," Dorothy said, sighing, "but we have to remember that the flaw is in his character, not ours. And apart from being good at bridge, what has he got? Who is more popular in the Club, you or him? You know it's you."

"I know, you're right. I suppose I have to be the bigger man." He took a sip of coffee. "I'll see you back inside."

Dorothy went to talk to the Tin Man. "You have to be nice to the Lion tonight," she told him. "He is feeling low and it will not do us any good to point out any of his mistakes. Okay?"

"Of course I'll be nice! But you know me: I say it as I see it — what's the harm in that?"

"The harm is that sometimes people are not interested in hearing it, and it won't improve our relationships. If you have something to say you can tell me later."

The Tin Man agreed, though he made it clear that he thought this was oversensitivity gone mad.

Soon the appointed moment came and the four of them were reunited at the table. Dorothy and the Scarecrow tried to say cheerful hellos. The Tin Man mumbled, and the Lion gave his quietest growl.

Dealer South. Both vul.

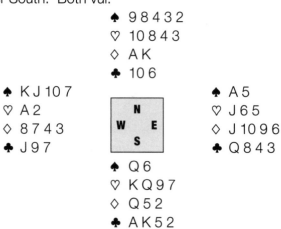

Dorothy dealt and opened One Heart, as dictated by their weak notrump, four-card major style. The Tin Man raised to Two Hearts and Dorothy had to decide whether or not to go on. As 16-counts go, this one seemed somehow lacking, but it was still 16. Her bid of Three Diamonds was a game-try, worried about losers in diamonds. With the ace-king of this suit, the Tin Man felt that he could not be faulted for accepting the invitation.

West	North	East	South
Lion	Tin Man	Scarecrow	Dorothy
			1♡
pass	2♡	pass	3◊
pass	4♡	all pass	

Hoping to play it safe and give nothing away, the Lion began the defense by leading the ◊7.

Dorothy could see that she had three top losers and the possibility of a second trump loser. She had five top tricks in the minors, with decent luck, meaning that she would need five tricks in the majors. Setting up spades was a possibility, but that would mean weakening her stronger trump holding, and drawing trumps might not be easy. A crossruff line looked more attractive, trumping clubs in the dummy and spades in hand. Putting this plan into action, she took two diamond winners in the dummy, crossed to the ♣A, cashed the ◊Q pitching a spade, cashed the ♣K, and ruffed a club in the dummy. When this had all passed off without incident, she called for a spade. The Scarecrow, who had already gone to bed with two aces that evening, flew in high, and when that scored he played a second spade, won by the Lion.

The Lion could see no defense to declarer's line of play if she was allowed to continue crossruffing, so he switched to ace and another heart. Putting the jack in would have given declarer the rest on a high crossruff, but the Scarecrow wisely, or fortunately, decided to hold it back, allowing dummy's eight of trumps to take the trick. That left these cards:

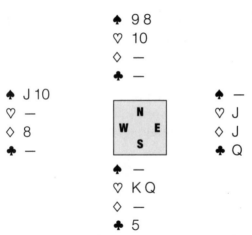

```
              ♠ 9 8
              ♡ 10
              ◇ —
              ♣ —

♠ J 10                        ♠ —
♡ —           ┌─────────┐     ♡ J
◇ 8           │    N    │     ◇ J
♣ —           │ W     E │     ♣ Q
              │    S    │
              └─────────┘
              ♠ —
              ♡ K Q
              ◇ —
              ♣ 5
```

The lead of a spade from dummy gave the Scarecrow an insoluble problem. If he ruffed, declarer would overruff and have a high crossruff. If he discarded a diamond, then declarer could ruff in hand, and ruff her losing club in dummy. If he discarded the ♣Q, then declarer's hand was high. In the end, he chose the diamond discard, on the grounds that he wasn't sure what was going on but that it seemed to be his least valuable card. Four Hearts making was a great score for North-South, as many people had not bid the game.

"Hmm," said the Tin Man. "Relying on the hand with the fourth club holding the jack of hearts. I'm not sure that was your best line but it was certainly a pretty ending. Oh, and there wasn't a thing that East-West could do, either in the bidding or the defense..." He paused, then said, "Which were exemplary."

The Lion shrugged his shoulders as if there had never been any other possibility. Taking care not to make eye contact with the Tin Man, he addressed the table in what he hoped sounded like a learned and philosophical tone.

"We just play our normal, tight game. That's all you can do. Some people worry about who they are playing, but what's the sense in that? Take your seat for the evening and play your game. Why waste energy thinking about who's coming your way? Sometimes you get your reward, sometimes they get lucky."

The Tin Man opened his mouth to reply, but shut it with a snap. He had caught sight of Dorothy's face. "Indeed so," he ventured after brief thought. "I'm sure we all agree with that."

11

The Odd Couple

The field had been getting smaller each year in the Club's Knockout Perfect Teams, an event in which each round would be a twenty-four-board match with the two captains sitting throughout and playing eight boards with each of their teammates. No one knew where the title came from. Some other clubs called this format Pivot Teams. It was rumored that a long since dead president of the former men's club, the Lollipop Guild, who had hailed from Australia, had created it.

Committee members had been encouraged to drum up teams to boost the numbers. Having had an ear battering from the Wicked Witch of the West, the Lion was on the prowl. The Scarecrow was eager to take part, and while it was good to have a second team member, choosing the Scarecrow did limit the people who were willing to take the third and fourth seats.

"I could ask Hank the Hunk," the Scarecrow suggested. The Lion shuddered. With Hank on board, the chances of completing the team with anyone outside of the beginners class were virtually non-existent.

He approached Dorothy in the hope that she might be able to persuade her aunt to join them. In a way this was a good thing, as it galvanized Auntie Em into rounding up and entering a team of her own.

As the search for a fourth player became increasingly desperate, the Lion gave in to Dorothy's suggestion that they ask the Tin Man. Dorothy managed to work her magic, and a team was formed, though the Tin Man made no secret of his feelings.

"Perfect, indeed," he had been heard muttering, "One partner is bad enough, but now I have to suffer several different fools all in one session." One thing he was sure of was that whatever happened during the event, he would hold the Lion responsible!

In the end, fourteen entries went into the hat. This meant there were six matches in the first round, with the Lion's team being one of the two with a bye. In the second round, they had been drawn against the winner of a match between the Chairman's four and a team that contained Hank the Hunk.

The Lion was worried about the match. Whichever team they faced, it would be a serious indignity to lose. He felt that he himself could manage the Scarecrow's eccentricities, but what about the eight boards to be played with each of Dorothy and the Tin Man? It would probably be all right with Dorothy, but could they avoid an explosion with the Tin Man having to cope with the Scarecrow's deficiencies for a full hour of bridge? The Lion decided that the team needed practice, but preferably in a way that kept them from interacting as much as possible. Bridge Base Online seemed the obvious solution.

And so, one evening, the four of them assembled together online, in the safety of their own homes. They had planned to start at seven thirty, but the game had been delayed while Dorothy was sent to search around the website for the Scarecrow. She eventually found him playing under an assumed name at a table with three Chinese players whom he had mistaken for his friends. She guided him to the correct table and they began.

Twenty minutes later, the Scarecrow was an unhappy man and wishing he was back at his previous table. They were on the fourth board, and he had already suffered a torrent of abuse from his partner, the Tin Man. It was all for such trivial reasons. They had defended the first two hands, and the Tin Man seemed to think that both contracts could have been beaten. He had tried an adventurous lead of a doubleton king on the first one. He had seen others do this, but how was he supposed to know this wouldn't be the right hand for it? Then on the second board, he had forgotten to cash the thirteenth spade when they already had four tricks defending Three Notrump. Finally, in a state of nervousness on Board 3, he had misclicked and passed his partner's opening with a 22-count. These things happened; surely partner could understand that? At least on BBO one couldn't revoke.

He was now about to declare the fourth hand. He had that inner feeling that whatever he did, the chat box on his screen would soon be full of pithy remarks, with more synonyms for "incompetent" and "idiot" than could be found in a good thesaurus.

Dealer South, E/W vul.

```
        ♠ 10 7 4 2
        ♡ A 8 5
        ◊ K 6
        ♣ K 10 9 5
        ┌──────────┐
        └──────────┘
        ♠ A K Q J
        ♡ 4 2
        ◊ Q 9 8 7 3 2
        ♣ 4
```

Dorothy had led the ♡Q after the following auction:

West	North	East	South
Dorothy	Tin Man	Lion	Scarecrow
			1◊
3♡	dbl*	pass	3♠
pass	4♠	all pass	

The Scarecrow would have bid Four Spades after his partner's double playing with the Lion. First, it was the probably the right value bid, and second, he knew that the Lion rarely raised an invitational bid. The Lion preferred to keep the auction low, especially when his partner was playing the hand.

Playing with the Tin Man, he wanted to bid what he would make. He felt the abuse would be less if he bid and made a partscore while missing game than if he bid a failing game. The Tin Man was made of sterner stuff than the Lion and, without sufficient experience playing with the Scarecrow, raised him to game.

The Scarecrow won the first trick with the ♡A, barely registering in his state of agitation that the Lion had played the king. He then started on the trumps. Both opponents followed to the first round, but then Dorothy discarded a heart on the second round.

Slowly it dawned on the Scarecrow that if he pulled all the trumps, he would have no protection against an avalanche of hearts. Clearly, he had to set up the diamond suit. He played the ♢2 and this went to Dorothy's ten, dummy's king and the Lion's ace. Back came a trump, Dorothy again discarding a heart.

Uncharacteristically, the Scarecrow had actually noticed Dorothy's card on the first round of diamonds. Could she have a doubleton J10? If so, his whole diamond suit would be good, and he would make his contract. He might get through one hand without complaint from his steely partner. Eagerly, he played the queen and then slumped back in his chair in disappointment when Dorothy threw yet another heart.

He had only one trump left in dummy and he needed to ruff diamonds twice. His contract would fail and Tinny would undoubtedly suggest improvements on what he had actually done at each and every trick. Whatever the layout, the Tin Man would have made it!

Despondently, the Scarecrow clicked the ♢7 and when Dorothy threw yet another heart, he clicked a heart also from dummy. The Lion won this with his jack and back came yet another trump.

Had he been at a bridge table, the Scarecrow would just have thrown in his cards and conceded one down, but he hadn't worked out yet how to claim on BBO. In the absence of anything better to do, he played off his diamonds. He saw Dorothy throw yet another heart and a couple of clubs, while the Lion threw a club. Before he played his last diamond, this was the position:

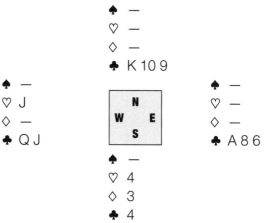

```
              ♠ —
              ♡ —
              ◇ —
              ♣ K 10 9
♠ —                          ♠ —
♡ J          ┌─────────┐     ♡ —
◇ —          │ N       │     ◇ —
♣ Q J        │ W     E │     ♣ A 8 6
             │    S    │
             └─────────┘
              ♠ —
              ♡ 4
              ◇ 3
              ♣ 4
```

The last diamond gave Dorothy a problem. If she discarded her heart, would the Scarecrow notice? Discarding a club was guaranteed to be fatal, so she discarded the heart. Sadly for Dorothy, but fortunately for the Scarecrow, the red four was closer to the Scarecrow's cursor than the black one.

The computer's made a mistake, thought the Scarecrow. It's showing this contract as making. Then he noticed an incoming comment from the Tin Man. He looked at it. It wasn't criticizing him. It actually said, "Well played, partner." It then went on in the Tin Man's usual sensitive manner, "You did very well to capitalize on the Lion's stupidity when he failed to cash the ace of clubs before exiting with his last trump. I thought we only had one cretin on the team."

In a daze, the Scarecrow looked at the new hand now facing him on the screen:

♠ A 9 2   ♡ K 9   ◇ Q 9   ♣ A Q 9 7 5 3

In his newfound confidence, he opened One Notrump. This was contrary to the team plan so clearly set out by the Tin Man. When the Scarecrow was partnering him, he was to avoid notrump openers wherever possible, as they made it too likely he would play the hand. To compound his felony, this hand did have a clear alternative opening bid. Three passes followed and he was in charge of the contract.

Dorothy led the ♣6 and dummy appeared:

♠ Q 10 5 4
♡ 10 7 6
♦ J 10 8 6 3
♣ J

▭

♠ A 9 2
♡ K 9
♦ Q 9
♣ A Q 9 7 5 3

Dummy won the first trick with the jack, after East, the Lion, contributed the two and the declarer played low.

The Scarecrow's mind wandered. He would really like to try to make some tricks in his six-card club suit, but no matter how hard he clicked on the ♣A, the computer wouldn't allow him to play it. Eventually, he realized it would only let him lead from dummy. He decided to try dummy's longest suit and played the ♦3. His queen was taken by Dorothy's king.

After a short pause for thought, Dorothy led the ♡2 to the Lion's ace, and another heart followed, which the Scarecrow won with the king. Having started on the diamond suit, he decided he might as well continue, so he led his remaining card and played dummy's jack, completely oblivious, of course, that the ♦9 and the ♦J were of equal value. The Lion won with the ace, and two rounds of hearts followed. The suit split 4-4, leaving Dorothy on lead. The Scarecrow had discarded the first small cards his cursor had landed on: two small clubs from his hand and the ♠4 from dummy.

Dorothy now played the ♠8, and the Scarecrow went into a state of deep contemplation. What he was contemplating was not clear, but it certainly wasn't the spade suit. A further vitriolic message from the Tin Man stirred him into action and he covered with the ten, which was itself covered by the Lion's jack and his own ace.

Well, he was sure he had clicked on the ace, but inexplicably the ♠9 had moved into the middle. He was desperate. The Tin Man's messages were already sounding murderous. What would he say now? Wait a minute. Wasn't there an undo button? Where was it; he searched frantically. Then he realized that a card had already appeared on the screen as the Lion led to the next trick after his unexpected success with the ♠J.

With five cards to go, the Lion had found himself on lead in this unappetizing situation:

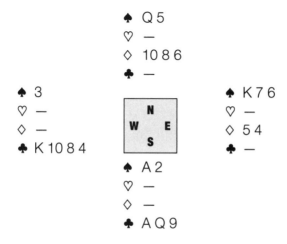

The Lion opted for a low spade. The Scarecrow played the two to keep control of the suit, and to his surprise found that the queen in dummy won the trick. He now played out three more rounds of diamonds, amazed to find them all winners; where had the ◊Q gone? It was probably an error in the BBO program. Seven tricks were his; three in diamonds, two in spades and one each in hearts and clubs.

The full hand was:

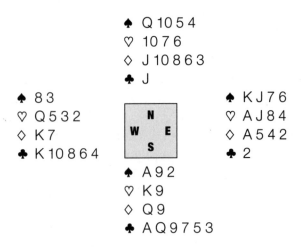

                    ♠ Q 10 5 4
                    ♡ 10 7 6
                    ◇ J 10 8 6 3
                    ♣ J

    ♠ 8 3   ♠ K J 7 6
    ♡ Q 5 3 2   N   ♡ A J 8 4
    ◇ K 7   W   E   ◇ A 5 4 2
    ♣ K 10 8 6 4   S   ♣ 2

                    ♠ A 9 2
                    ♡ K 9
                    ◇ Q 9
                    ♣ A Q 9 7 5 3

"Well played, Scarecrow" came the chat message from Dorothy.

"You may have saved yourself in the play, but bid like that again and you shall not be forgiven" was all the Tin Man could muster.

The Lion sat back in his seat. Coming from the Tin Man, that was practically a compliment! Perhaps this team might work out well after all!

 Diamonds Are Forever

It was a bright day in early August. The roses were in full bloom, the trees were green, and the weather was warm and dry. It was a time to savor, a time to be lively and cheerful.

The Lion looked through the window of his front room at this happy scene with his legs trembling. Tonight would see the first real action for his team in the Perfect Teams knockout. They would be playing the team led by the Honorary Chairman of the Lollipop Guild. That certainly didn't worry him. They had only beaten the team that included Hank the Hunk in the first round; all that proved was that they had shown up.

The Chairman would have the Mayor of Munchkinland on his team. Both of them were sound but uninspiring players, as were the two other Munchkins who completed his lineup.

The Lion felt a bit like the Duke of Wellington. He didn't know what effect his team would have on the opposition, but it certainly scared him. Well, at least one member of the team did. The Tin Man had made it abundantly clear that he considered this form of team game somewhat less than perfect. To prepare him for the mind-numbing experience of partnering the Scarecrow for eight boards, the team had arranged a second BBO practice session. After all, the first had passed off quite well; the Scarecrow's random play of the cards had come up lucky every time. Unfortunately, the fairy godmother who had protected him on the first occasion had apparently taken the evening off on the second.

The Lion could remember with total clarity his conversation with the Tin Man when they met at the club the following evening. Actually, "conversation" would not really be the correct description, as he could not recall contributing a single word, such was the torrent directed at him.

"How did I ever get into this situation?" ... "I'll hold you personally responsible" ... "The man is clueless..."

And now the Lion had his captaincy duties to consider. He would be sitting East throughout in one room, with the Chairman on his right as North. The other three members of their respective teams would come in for eight boards each in the South and West seats.

The strongest lineup would be for him to play with the Scarecrow, with Dorothy partnering the Tin Man in the other room. Ideally, he thought he would have wanted to save this lineup for the last set, just in case they needed to pull in something special then. However, that would mean the Tin Man playing with the Scarecrow at an earlier stage. With steam coming out of his ears at the end of these eight boards, would he be able to concentrate on the remainder of the match?

No! That partnership had to be left to the end. The best scenario would see the opponents concede after two sets. The second-best scenario would see his team concede. The nightmare scenario was that the match would go the distance. He made the decision; they would start with the strongest pairings and hope to build up a big lead.

The club had two small rooms for head-to-head team matches. After the usual pleasantries among seven of the members of the teams, the Lion and the Chairman took their seats in the Indigo Room. The Tin Man was already seated in the Violet Room. They were about to draw the cards out of the first board when the door of the Indigo Room opened.

"You won't mind if I watch?" asked the Wicked Witch of the West in her sweetest cackle. "As we'll be playing the winner of tonight's match, I thought I would take the opportunity to assess the opposition."

The Lion shifted uncomfortably as the Witch pulled up a chair behind him. Things were quiet until the fourth board appeared on the table:

Dealer West. Both vul.

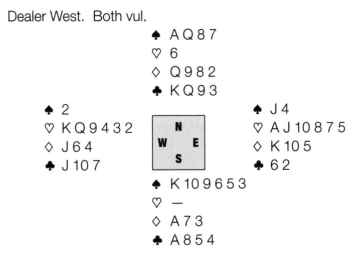

```
                    ♠ A Q 8 7
                    ♡ 6
                    ◇ Q 9 8 2
                    ♣ K Q 9 3
    ♠ 2                             ♠ J 4
    ♡ K Q 9 4 3 2         N        ♡ A J 10 8 7 5
    ◇ J 6 4          W        E    ◇ K 10 5
    ♣ J 10 7              S        ♣ 6 2
                    ♠ K 10 9 6 5 3
                    ♡ —
                    ◇ A 7 3
                    ♣ A 8 5 4
```

The Scarecrow, sitting West, opened Two Hearts, an unusually accurate description of his hand. The Chairman doubled, and the Lion went into a huddle. He had a clear preemptive raise in Hearts, but to what level? He knew that holding hearts with the opposition clearly having a spade fit, he should go to the five-level... but they were vulnerable. After a full three minutes, he emerged with Four Hearts.

The Munchkin in the South seat was made of sterner stuff and jumped to Five Spades, and the Chairman, propped up on three cushions to give him a clear view of the table, raised to the slam.

The auction had been:

West	North	East	South
Scarecrow	Chairman	Lion	Munchkin
2♡	dbl	4♡	5♠
pass	6♠	all pass	

Leading was the part of the game that the Scarecrow found easiest. There were such straightforward rules, he thought to himself, as he pulled out the fourth highest of his longest suit and laid it face down on the table. The Lion indicated no questions and he turned it over. He stared at it. It was a remarkably pointed heart. Panicking, he looked at his hand. Sure enough, there was a remarkably rounded four sitting in his diamond suit.

Declarer stared at the ♢4 sitting on the table. What had West led from? If it was a singleton or a small doubleton, the contract was unmakeable now. It was unlikely to be from a suit headed by both the jack and ten. So if it was a lead from one of the jack or ten, East would play the other, and he would still be on a guess later in the hand as to where the king was. Then he spotted the best line. Playing the queen gave him a double chance. It would work if the lead was away from the king, but would also work if the lead was from a four-card suit headed by the jack or ten, as East, with a doubleton KJ or K10 would be endplayed towards the end of the hand to give a ruff and discard.

He proceeded with his plan and drifted one down. "Sorry partner," he mumbled, "that was a difficult lead to read."

Half an hour later, they finished the set and, followed by the Wicked Witch, went to join their teammates who had been waiting for a full five minutes.

"Call your scores," ordered the Tin Man.

"Plus 400," said the Lion.

"Minus an IMP," intoned the Tin Man. "There were only ten tricks on top."

"Minus 140."

"Another IMP away — five top winners on defense."

"Minus 120."

"And another — just six top winners this time."

"Plus 100."

"Plus 17! I thought my endplay would bring the IMPs in. After the routine heart lead, I cleared the trumps and the clubs, and played a diamond to the nine. I was fairly sure the Munchkin wouldn't manage that!"

"Actually, it wasn't like that," said the Lion, "My partner found the inspired lead of a small diamond. Perfectly reasonably, declarer played the queen from dummy and that was the end of the hand."

"That's a brilliant lead, Scarecrow," said Dorothy. "The only one to give him a problem. How did you find it?"

"Er, well, it's all this reading I've been doing," muttered the Scarecrow. "I'm sure there was a hand just like that in, what's his name, Bill Lawrence... or, umm, er, was it Kelsey Matheson... or it might have been in Bridge Magazine?

"Hee, hee," cackled the Wicked Witch. "I am sure the Lion and the Scarecrow were expecting to win sixteen IMPs rather than seventeen. They would have hoped that any semi-competent pair would reach the far superior Six Clubs."

After a few more small losses were scored up, they had won the set by 10 IMPs, the only difference being that the Tin Man was silent for the rest of the scoring.

The boards of the second session were quiet, and the Scarecrow could throw only 5 IMPs. However, Dorothy had made a Three Notrump contract on a double squeeze not found in the other room. So going into the final session with the Scarecrow and the Tin Man in harness, they were 15 IMPs up.

Almost an hour later, the last board was put on the table in the Violet Room. The Scarecrow tried to take his cards out. That was easier said than done by this stage of the event. He had been lambasted for seven boards and was shaking violently. He had gone down in a Three Notrump contract. In reality, he had had no option but to open One Notrump, and despite his misgivings, the Tin Man had raised him to game with his 15-count. The Tin Man seemed to think that ten tricks were easy, but the defense had somehow cashed five. And then there was the Four Spades they had defended, when he had revoked on the second round of trumps. Not only did that cost a trick, but as the revoke card was the ace of trumps, it was difficult not to be penalized a second trick.

It was clear the match was in the balance, as he sorted his cards to see this hand:

♠A ♡KQ10642 ◇AQ42 ♣A2

It was also clear to the Wicked Witch, who was kibitzing against the Scarecrow. Astutely, she knew which of the four players she was most likely to put off, and had taken her seat accordingly. She was fairly sure her low-level humming had played a part in the Scarecrow's play of that Three Notrump, and she was proud of her loud burp immediately prior to the revoke.

The Scarecrow added up his points. Three aces made 12; then 5 points in hearts made 17; the ◇Q made 19; and the ♠A made a total of 23. He opened Two Clubs and heard partner give a positive response with Three Clubs. He showed his heart suit at the three-level, but partner pushed on with Four Clubs.

Bouncing with excitement, he bid Four Notrump. The Tin Man assumed that they were playing Roman Keycard Blackwood and endeavored to show one of the five aces. Thinking that he had located the ♡A, the Scarecrow drove forward with Five Notrump to check on kings. The Tin Man took this to be a grand slam try holding all of the keycards. He felt confident that his hand fully justified a leap to Seven

Clubs. West's double card was the first sign that they might not be on the same wavelength.

The Tin Man was endplayed. There was nothing he could do to help. The Scarecrow had bid both clubs and notrump first, apparently the only two possible denominations for the hand, so whatever he did, he would have to sit and watch the massacre and the end of their participation in the event — which was, at least, a silver lining. For seven boards, he had been coaxing his partner along with good advice and this was how he was rewarded!

The Wicked Witch was beaming from ear to ear. To make sure of a good penalty, she started her low-level humming again, sticking with a winning formula.

The full hand was:

Dealer South. Both vul.

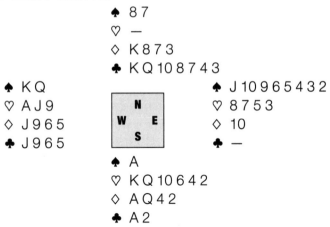

	♠	8 7
	♡	—
	◇	K 8 7 3
	♣	K Q 10 8 7 4 3

♠ K Q	♠ J 10 9 6 5 4 3 2
♡ A J 9	♡ 8 7 5 3
◇ J 9 6 5	◇ 10
♣ J 9 6 5	♣ —

	♠	A
	♡	K Q 10 6 4 2
	◇	A Q 4 2
	♣	A 2

West	North	East	South
Chairman	*Tin Man*	*Munchkin*	*Scarecrow*
			2♣
pass	3♣	pass	3♡
pass	4♣	pass	4NT
pass	5◇	pass	5NT
pass	7♣	pass	pass
dbl	all pass		

The Chairman thought for a minute, then led his ♠K. Winning this, the Scarecrow led out the ♡K, ruffing when the ace was played. Eager to get back to his hand to cash a winning heart, he played the king of trumps, then a trump to the ace, at this point noticing that East's black card was a spade, and he realized that he had no idea whether East had followed suit on the first round of trumps.

The Scarecrow was in panic mode. He felt sure that he was on the verge of losing the match single-handedly. If the previous hands were not bad enough, he had bid a grand slam not realizing there was an ace missing: it was sheer good fortune that dummy had been void in that suit. And now he had lost count of the trumps!

He knew only two things for certain. First, he was entirely responsible. But worse still, he knew that the Tin Man knew that he was. He could already hear the forthcoming postmatch discussion playing over and over in his head. He just wanted to go home and go to bed!

Not wanting to strain himself further by thinking, he cashed the ♡Q and ruffed a heart in dummy. By now, he had no idea what cards remained in any suit. Returning to hand with the ◊Q, he played the ♡4 and saw West play a red six on it. The Scarecrow ruffed and decided to try to cash his diamonds, playing the king and then the ace.

With the lead in his hand at Trick 11, the position was:

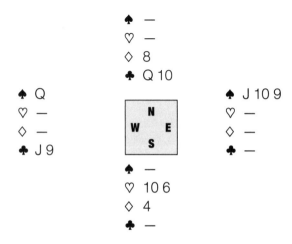

Hoping simply to get two more ruffs and only go one down, the Scarecrow played the ♡10. The Chairman threw his cards on the table and held his head in his hands.

"Why did I, oh why did I d- d- discard that six of d- d- diamonds?" he cried. "That will be 2330!"

The Scarecrow was shocked. That seemed a huge penalty and a peculiar one, not being a round number of hundreds! As there were only three tricks left, he couldn't go more than three down. It took a full thirty seconds before he realized that his grand slam was being conceded. He didn't want to take a contract that wasn't rightly his, but he had learned over the years not to question players better than him. That meant he rarely disputed such things.

He noticed that the low hum that had been irritating him seemed to have stopped as the Wicked Witch stomped out of the room. Then he noticed that it had been replaced by a slow hiss that seemed to be emanating from the direction of his otherwise speechless partner.

"That was a bit tighter than I had expected," said the Lion, exuding confidence and composure once they had scored up. "We'll all have to be on better form for the witches in the next round. Now, have you got your diaries so we can find a few dates I can offer them?"

Toil and Trouble

The witches were plotting.

That evening they would be playing the semifinal of the Club's Pivot Teams event, known, most would say jokingly, as the Perfect Teams. The two captains, the Irritable Witch of the South and the Lion, would sit at the same table for all twenty-four boards as South and East respectively. They would then play three sets of eight boards partnering each of their teammates in turn.

"Can you imagine Old Tinny sitting opposite that half-stuffed, idiot Scarecrow?" cackled the Wicked Witch.

"He will have that Scarecrow not knowing which way is up by the end of the eight boards," shrieked the Irritable Witch of the South.

"And we can certainly assist him," giggled the Unpleasant Witch of the North. "A little bit of hubble-bubble, toil and trouble, brewed up and stirred well, and we'll be unlucky not to get 50 IMPs out of that set."

"In the previous round, the Lion played that combination for the final set," the Wicked Witch added thoughtfully. "He will probably do the same again, hoping the match is effectively over before he has to field his nightmare pairing."

"So what we want is for you and me, Wicked," the Unpleasant Witch chuckled to herself, "to deal with them. We'll sort them out."

"Yes, indeed," muttered the Irritable Witch. "Glinda would be far too soft on them. I'm sure I can rely on the two of you to get them going."

They cackled the afternoon away. The result, they felt, was a foregone conclusion.

For the first session of the match, both teams had their most regular pairings playing. The only serious swing occurred when the Tin Man made a Three Notrump contract on a misdefense from Glinda and a squeeze. In the other room, the Irritable Witch of the South also had the benefit of a misdefense, courtesy of the Scarecrow, but she made the serious mistake of believing that the Scarecrow's play might be rational, leading to her taking a good but failing line.

This delighted the Unpleasant Witch of the North. Double-dummy analysis was her specialty, and hands played by her partner that failed, but could be made if her partner had the foresight of Deep Finesse, were a great source of material for future aggravation. The team being down by 8 IMPs after this set was a small price to pay for the subsequent pleasure this hand would give her.

She was even happier after the second set. The Lion, now partnering the Tin Man, had failed to add 3 points for his partner's play and had missed a game that was bid and made at the other table. And then on the last hand of the set, the Scarecrow had revoked instead of playing the ace of trumps. He had just realized he would shortly be playing with the Tin Man and in his panic didn't even hear Dorothy's "Having none, partner?"

The witches had won the set by 22 IMPs. "We're leading by 14 IMPs, and they've still to play the Scarecrow partnering Tinny," the Unpleasant Witch of the North chortled. "I wonder if they'll play the last set."

The Lion had his head in his hands and was having very similar thoughts. Dorothy took his arm. "It's not going well, but let's play it out," she said comfortingly. "With a bit of luck, we'll be able to pick up some points in our room, and with even more luck, the hands in the other room will be played by the Tin Man."

One the first hand of the set, the Tin Man, sitting North, was presented with a tactical bidding problem. He held:

♠ A 10 9 3   ♡ J 10 6 4 3   ♢ —   ♣ A 10 9 6

The Scarecrow, as dealer, opened One Diamond and then rebid One Notrump over his One Heart response. He tried Two Clubs, Checkback, consoling himself that if his idiot partner didn't remember they were playing this convention, he at least did have a club suit.

The Scarecrow now bid Two Notrump, and this was where the problem arose. What could he possibly do to avoid the Scarecrow playing the hand? After a long hesitation, he gave up and bid Three Notrump, which became the final contract. The auction, with both sides vulnerable, had been:

West	North	East	South
Wicked	Tin Man	Unpleasant	Scarecrow
			1◇
pass	1♡	pass	1NT
pass	2♣*	pass	2NT
pass	3NT	all pass	

The Wicked Witch of the West interrogated the Scarecrow about the meaning of the auction and then led the ◇3. Much to the Tin Man's surprise, the Scarecrow had remembered the system.

As dummy was being laid down, the Unpleasant Witch took the opportunity to stir things up. "I thought you said the Two Club bid was artificial. He's got a club suit."

"Oh yes, em, well, er, he might not have had, or perhaps he should have had, or em, perhaps not, um..." After thirty seconds of this, the Scarecrow was totally confused. He looked at his hand and tried to construct a line of play that was not likely to cause his partner to explode:

♠ A 10 9 3
♡ J 10 6 4 3
◊ —
♣ A 10 9 6

```
┌──────────┐
└──────────┘
```

♠ J 8 7
♡ Q 2
◊ A K Q 8 6
♣ K J 4

It so happened that the auction had been the same in the other room. Once again, the ◊3 was led, and as dummy went down in the Three Notrump contract, the Irritable Witch of the South realized she had to make an awkward decision at Trick 1 as to what to discard from dummy. If she tried to set up the hearts, she was in danger of losing three tricks in the suit. If the defense managed to get a long diamond and a spade, the contract would be down. Playing on the black suits, she just needed one of three finesses to work, with the added advantage that the club finesse could be taken either way. She discarded a heart.

When the Lion, sitting East, played the ◊10, Irritable won the first trick with the ace and ran the ♠J, losing to the queen. She won the second diamond trick with the king, discarding another heart, and tried another spade finesse, losing to the king.

The Lion now played the two top hearts and a third heart won by the jack, the suit splitting 3-3. She had lost four tricks, so needed all the rest in the following position:

♠ A 10
♡ —
◇ —
♣ A 10 9 6
<hr>
♠ 8
♡ —
◇ Q 8
♣ K J 4

It all depended on doing the right thing in clubs. East had shown up with 12 points in the major suits. With the ♣Q as well, surely even the Lion would have been tempted to enter the auction. She cashed her two spade winners, the Lion following to both. She now knew that East had started with four spades and three hearts. Dorothy's lead of the ◇3 with the ◇2 played subsequently implied the diamonds were split 5-3, but the Lion's failure to continue a third round of diamonds suggested he might have started with only two of them. So his shape was either 4=3=3=3 or 4=3=2=4. Counting the cards told her that if either defender had greater length in clubs, it was surely the Lion, but counting high cards seemed to put the ♣Q in Dorothy's hand: surely, if he had it, the Lion would have had a routine double after Glinda's One Heart response?

With her mind made up, Irritable returned to hand with the ♣K and played her ◇Q and then another club, expecting the queen to show up. Dorothy smiled inwardly as the Irritable Witch went one down. Dorothy knew exactly how South had planned the hand, but she also had the advantage of knowing how the Lion bid.

```
♠ A 10 9 3
♡ J 10 6 4 3
♢ —
♣ A 10 9 6
┌────────┐
└────────┘
♠ J 8 7
♡ Q 2
♢ A K Q 8 6
♣ K J 4
```

The Scarecrow was now faced with the same problem at Trick 1 as the Irritable Witch. His thinking processes were limited at the best of times, but with two very nasty opponents and seven more boards to play with the Tin Man, the Scarecrow's mind was close to panic. After a brief struggle, his brain correctly diagnosed this as a hand that was too hard for him to work out. Saving power for the remainder of the set, he looked at the lead: he saw that it was a red card so he played a red card from dummy.

Focusing briefly before he played from hand (he was under orders to keep revokes to a minimum), he ascertained that the lead was a diamond. He won it with the ace. With no clear plan in mind, he now played his ♠J, running it to the Unpleasant Witch in the East seat. She won this with the king. Foolishly, she thought that by not playing the queen she might encourage him to take another finesse. Such plays only work against declarers who are aware what card has been played.

The Unpleasant Witch now returned the ♢7. Completely at a loss as to what had happened two tricks earlier, the Scarecrow played the eight, and the Wicked Witch of the West won the trick with the nine, another heart being discarded from dummy.

The Wicked Witch stared at this trick and tried to work out the diamond suit. The play made sense only if her partner had started with 1076. Also, it was clear to her that the Scarecrow, having the ♠Q, had three spade tricks and three diamond tricks. This was surely the time to be passive, so she returned another diamond.

The Scarecrow threw a club from dummy, for variety, and was so astonished to win the trick with his six that he didn't notice the Wicked Witch's heartfelt curse. He was about to take another spade finesse when he actually had a thought. A check of the cards in front of the other three players confirmed his suspicion that he had lost two tricks and there was still the small matter of the ♡AK. If he took a finesse and it failed, that would be the end of his contract. He looked across the table. It wasn't difficult to tell that there was steam coming out of the Tin Man's ears.

The bonus diamond trick gave him four in that suit, and he had three top tricks in the black suits. Just two more to go! There was one sure way to set up a trick without any danger, so he played his ♡Q. The Unpleasant Witch won this, cashed the other top heart, and played a third one, won by dummy's jack.

The Scarecrow was now looking at the following cards, needing all the remaining tricks:

♠ A 10 9
♡ —
◇ —
♣ A 10 9

♠ 8
♡ —
◇ K Q
♣ K J 4

The Scarecrow had lost track of what cards had been played. As long as he managed not to block himself, he believed that he could get out for down one. Yes, that should be possible. He played the ♣A, and then a club to his king so that he could take his two top diamonds, throwing one of each of dummy's black suits.

At this point, two extraordinary things happened. The Unpleasant Witch on his right, who was wriggling uncomfortably, reduced to the ♠Q5 and the ♣Q, threw the club, hoping that her partner could guard the suit. But even more surprising, the Scarecrow was aware that this meant that his jack was a master.

She's supposed to be a good player, he thought to himself, and she can still make stupid errors like that. Maybe she finds playing with the Wicked Witch as scary as I find playing with the Tin Man.

He was so deep in thought that he never heard the Tin Man say, "Well done, partner... I think."

The full hand had been:

Dealer South. Both vul.

```
                      ♠ A 10 9 3
                      ♥ J 10 6 4 3
                      ◇ —
                      ♣ A 10 9 6
        ♠ 6 2                        ♠ K Q 5 4
        ♥ 9 8 7         N            ♥ A K 5
        ◇ J 9 5 3 2   W   E          ◇ 10 7 4
        ♣ 8 7 3         S            ♣ Q 5 2
                      ♠ J 8 7
                      ♥ Q 2
                      ◇ A K Q 8 6
                      ♣ K J 4
```

The Scarecrow played the next six hands in something of a daze. Fortunately, his partner was declarer in three of them and his own scope for self-harm was limited to conceding four gratuitous overtricks in the other three. The Tin Man had entered robot mode, doing his best to avoid unnecessary engagement with the other three players and ignoring the efforts of the witches to irritate him. Playing quickly suited the Scarecrow too. He was counting down the boards, feeling a growing sense of relief as each one was completed and entered into his scorecard.

Play was not going so quickly in the other room. Glinda was at her most spellbinding and the Irritable Witch of the South was delighted with the distracting effect that this was having on the Lion and the growing frustration that it was causing Dorothy. Bewitching one of the opponents in this manner was not an approach used by her and her regular partner, the Unpleasant Witch of the North. However, it seemed to be effective at giving them that extra edge, so she decided to sit back and see how much advantage could be gained.

The Lion rose to the occasion, hanging on every tinkling laugh, blushing at every winning smile, and insisting on fetching Glinda first water, then coffee, and then painstakingly relocating the table by a matter of inches in order to provide her with better lighting.

"Oh, thank you so much!" She beamed at him. "Now I can see so much better."

"And more importantly, we can see you so much better, too!" the Lion purred.

Dorothy, feeling nauseated, tried to break the spell. "Come on folks, we are well behind time here. They've already taken our other three boards and they will want this one soon."

In her hurry to restart play, Dorothy put the next board on the table the wrong way round, making Glinda South.

Dealer East. Both vul.

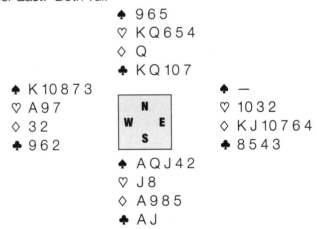

Glinda found herself declarer in Four Spades, much to the disgust of the Irritable Witch, who felt both robbed of a good hand and worried by what Glinda might do with it.

The Lion, now with the West cards, led the ◊3 to the queen, king, and ace. Glinda played two rounds of clubs, ending in dummy, then called for a trump. When East showed out, she looked disappointed and took the known losing finesse to the Lion's king. The Lion played a second diamond and Glinda did the best she could by ruffing. She tried a heart to her jack. The Lion won the ace and delicately laid down the ♠10, pinning dummy's nine.

The remaining cards were:

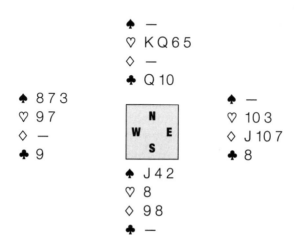

Dummy was bursting with winners but the Lion could not be denied two more trump tricks.

"I'm sorry, my dear," the Lion spoke softly, comforting Glinda by patting her hand. "You were so very unlucky."

Dorothy grabbed the board and took it through to the other room, as much to escape from the table for a few seconds as anything else. She passed it to the Tin Man, who placed it, mechanically, in the center of the table.

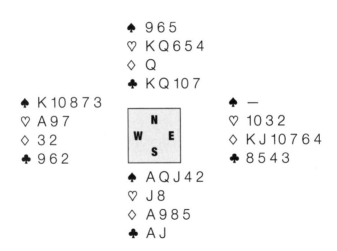

```
              ♠ 9 6 5
              ♡ K Q 6 5 4
              ◊ Q
              ♣ K Q 10 7
♠ K 10 8 7 3      N        ♠ —
♡ A 9 7       W       E    ♡ 10 3 2
◊ 3 2             S        ◊ K J 10 7 6 4
♣ 9 6 2                    ♣ 8 5 4 3
              ♠ A Q J 4 2
              ♡ J 8
              ◊ A 9 8 5
              ♣ A J
```

The Unpleasant Witch, sitting as dealer in the East seat, opened Two Diamonds in front of the Scarecrow. He turned to the Wicked Witch and asked what this meant.

She saw this as a last opportunity to rattle the Scarecrow further. "What do you think? We're at the last board of a twenty-four-board match and all our pairings are playing that as a weak two. Can you not read?" She thrust a grubby card in front of him.

"I'm very sorry," muttered the Scarecrow, and then he mumbled, "Two Spades."

"In case you haven't noticed," said the Wicked Witch, delighted with the way things were going, "we're using bidding boxes. Well, at least three of us are."

Feeling very flustered, the Scarecrow pulled out the Two Spade bid and placed it on the table.

The Tin Man had feared this sort of situation. He had the values for game but his three small spades were not the sort of support he would feel comfortable laying down for this partner. Perhaps Three Notrump would be better than Four Spades, if he could arrange to play it?

He looked across the table. Despite his best efforts to be the perfect partner, it was only too clear that the Scarecrow had managed to work himself up into an absurdly agitated state. If he started a constructive sequence, there was every chance that he would find himself passed out in a partscore.

With only a singleton queen in the opponents' suit, it would be difficult to justify his normal solution to this type of problem — simply bidding Three Notrump. Make that a doubleton queen, and he would have no qualms!

The best of a series of bad options was to bid Four Spades, even with the Scarecrow playing it. With any luck, they would have so many values that wrong-siding the contract would cost only overtricks.

The full auction had been:

West	North	East	South
Wicked	*Tin Man*	*Unpleasant*	*Scarecrow*
		2◊	2♠
pass	4♠	all pass	

The Wicked Witch selected the ◊3 as her lead. After a minute watching the Scarecrow trying to balance the thirteen cards in his hand, the Tin Man made an executive decision and played the ◊Q, covered quickly by the king. Even this didn't seem to spark the Scarecrow into action.

"We would like to finish by midnight," said the Wicked Witch. "Perhaps you might consider playing from your hand. Four is the traditional number of cards in a trick!"

The Scarecrow jumped. "Oh, I'm sorry, I, em..." he warbled, as he pulled out the ◊A, simultaneously dropping the ♠2 on the table.

The Wicked Witch pounced on this with the ten. "You've at least accelerated the speed of play," she chuckled.

"What happened?" said the dizzy Scarecrow.

"Clearly, you won the ace of diamonds and then led your small spade at Trick 2," the Wicked Witch replied. "And now I've covered it with the ten."

"It hardly matters," grated the Tin Man through clenched teeth. "It's unlikely to improve matters if you think about the cards you're playing." Despite the lack of an instruction from the Scarecrow, he helped himself to dummy's smallest spade and then shuddered when he saw the Unpleasant Witch discard a diamond.

The Wicked Witch continued with the ◊2, which the Scarecrow ruffed in dummy.

Three tricks had been played, and the Scarecrow had a thought that made him smile. Only ten more tricks and his eight boards with The Tin Man would be over. He looked at his hand and at dummy, elated by the prospect of this nightmare coming to an end.

It must be a good idea to knock out the ♡A, he thought, so he played up to the jack in his hand. The Wicked Witch of the West won this with her ace and played back the ♡7; the Scarecrow won in the dummy.

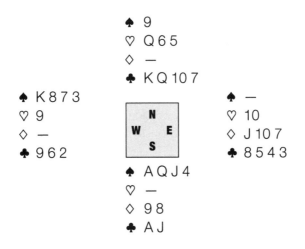

The Scarecrow cashed another top heart, pitching a diamond, then three top clubs, throwing his last diamond, the Wicked Witch following suit to each trick with increasing disgust. His last four cards were all trumps. He had forgotten to pull them. Afraid to look at the Tin Man, he played the ♠9. East's discard came as a shock to him. He hadn't noticed her showing out on the first round of trumps. But then, to his surprise, the Wicked Witch threw her cards on the table.

"One more to me," she croaked.

"Ten tricks," said the Tin Man, sweeping up dummy and putting the Scarecrow's cards away for him. He knew that had the Scarecrow been left to play out the hand, he would probably have been unaware that the ♠10 had gone and would have done something fatal like putting in the ♠Q. It was always so much easier when defenders assumed that the Scarecrow was going to play semi-competently. Finally, he gathered up his bewildered partner and walked him out of the room.

The Unpleasant Witch was apoplectic. "What made you win the first trump?" she shrieked. "Let him win in dummy, and who knows what will happen. At least you will keep your trump strength. Even better, don't force him to play a spade at Trick 2! How could that be a good idea?"

The Wicked Witch shifted uncomfortably. "Don't be ridiculous. He can still make it easily enough," she said defensively.

"I certainly would," screamed the Unpleasant Witch, "and at the top of your form you might also. But would he?" She pointed at the departing Scarecrow. "When did you last look to him for a rational line of play?"

It took another half-hour for the other table to finish. Much to the disappointment of the Irritable Witch, the Lion's response to Glinda's allure had been to play some of his most dashing, or at least less stodgy, bridge, basking in the attention of this divine creature.

The Lion stalked slowly out of the room feeling jubilant. He thought that he might be in love. To add to that, his team had won by 2 IMPs.

"It's Auntie Em next in the final," he said, bouncing. "Let's see if we can find some dates to give her." Without thinking further, he left his teammates in order to see if Glinda might need a lift home.

Dorothy took out her diary before she realized the Lion had gone. The Tin Man and the Scarecrow both stared vacantly into the space ahead of them. For once the two had the same thought: "Another eight boards with him!"

A Room with a View

"We'll use the Indigo Room as the Closed Room," boomed Auntie Em authoritatively, "and we can use the Violet Room as the Open Room since it is bigger. The captains will, of course, play in the Open Room throughout." She looked around. About a dozen Club members had come along on a sunny September evening to spectate.

It was the final of the Club's Pivot teams, when the two captains would sit throughout at the same table, playing eight boards in partnership with each of their teammates. It had been known as the Perfect Teams for as long as anyone could remember, a title that had provoked more jokes than any other subject in human memory. Even Munchkin Bob had run out of new ideas for wisecracks on it, but he was happy to recycle old ones.

"Can we not have both rooms open?" cackled the Unpleasant Witch of the North. "As long as no spectator can enter a playing room after the start of an eight-board session, what harm can come of it?" The match was a win-win situation for her: a team that she didn't like was going to lose, and she was hoping to pick up material that she could cast up against both teams.

"That would be most irregular," creaked the Tin Man.

"I wouldn't want that either," said Dorothy, looking thoughtful. "I think we should do exactly as Auntie Em suggested." She knew perfectly well what was in the minds of the three witches. What an opportunity it would be for creating chaos with a few well-chosen comments when the Tin Man partnered the Scarecrow! But with the Lion as captain in the Open Room, this partnership would be out of sight in the Closed Room.

The Lion had already decided to keep to the lineup that had worked in the previous two matches. He would start with his two regular partnerships and keep the nightmare partnership of the Tin Man and the Scarecrow to the last set. With luck, they could build up a lead in the first two sets. He knew Auntie Em would never concede even if she needed 20 IMPs on each board, but at least he could hope that he might have a margin large enough to be Scarecrow-proof.

Auntie Em had been giving the match considerable thought. She had no worries about any of her partnerships. They were a well-tried team used to playing in different pairings. Furthermore, any partnership with her in it was strong and should easily compensate for minor problems at the other table.

However, she knew the problem the Lion was facing, and she also knew how he had chosen to line up in earlier matches. Someone as cautious as the Lion would surely keep to his winning formula. If she herself was at the table facing this partnership of the Tin Man and the Scarecrow, she felt sure she could inflict severe damage.

The Lion won the toss and took the North seat. It provided the most comfortable seating for spectators, allowing Cissie and Ada to place themselves behind each of his shoulders. Glinda sat behind the Scarecrow and smiled encouragingly at the Lion. It came as a surprise when Uncle Henry and Hickory came in to take the East and West seats, respectively.

"Shouldn't your captain be in this room?" the Lion queried.

"I've just been informed that I've been made captain," said Uncle Henry in a tone that made it clear that he had been told this by she who must be obeyed.

The Unpleasant Witch of the North cackled. "Yes, old Em has launched a coup against herself and installed a puppet regime." Henry visibly stiffened, but made no comment.

The first eight boards saw the Lion and Zeke in the North seat in each of the two rooms, leading to some serious underbidding. With the cards lying their way, this meant that even the Scarecrow made the two contracts on which he was declarer. With two slams and three games missed at each table,

leaving their East and West teammates confident of gains in the scoring up, the set was decided by the Scarecrow calculating four kings as 14 points, thus ensuring that they bid a combined 25-count to Three Notrump. The Unpleasant Witch of the North was smiling broadly. She had seen enough bad play to justify writing an article for the Club magazine that would be sure to upset everyone.

The Lion's team led by 12 IMPs after this set. Dorothy smiled, as she could not avoid hearing the other team scoring up. Zeke was being well and truly roasted by Auntie Em. He would be very unlikely to underbid quite so much in the next set.

Luck ran out for the Lion's team in the second set. Despite Dorothy's best endeavors, she couldn't avoid the Scarecrow playing three boards, all in game contracts. The good news was that one of them was a Three Notrump with eleven on top, so they lost only 2 IMPs when the Scarecrow stumbled upon an endplay to rescue the ninth trick. The other two didn't stretch Auntie Em in the other room, but when the Scarecrow played for the deck to contain fifteen hearts on one of them, and for South to hold a 4-4-4-3 distribution on the other, problems did arise.

The net result of the second set was a loss for the Lion's team by 17 IMPs, which was a relief to Dorothy, who had feared it might be more. They trailed by 5 IMPs going into the fateful final set.

Auntie Em took the South seat in the Closed Room, hovering over the table like a large spider watching flies approach its web. Hickory sat opposite her with a broad smile on his face. With 5 IMPs in the bag and a pair coming to sit East-West more akin to Laurel and Hardy than a bridge partnership, he was confident he was going to enjoy these eight boards.

The first six boards turned out to be fairly quiet. The Scarecrow had relatively little to do. He did fail to make a takeout double of Auntie Em's One Club opener on a 14-count with both majors. Instead of making their own partscore, they had to content themselves with Auntie Em going one down. Auntie Em mentally registered another 3 IMP gain, while the Tin Man explained to the Scarecrow how to count his points and the merits of his making a takeout double, as it increased the chances of his partner playing the hand.

Then there was the hand when the Scarecrow had failed to double holding ♣AKQJ10, on lead against Auntie Em's vulnerable Three Notrump. Merely 3 IMPs, thought Auntie Em, but after three full minutes of the Tin Man giving his opinions on the Scarecrow's sanity, she was aware, as the seventh board was put on the table, that her left-hand opponent was close to buckling under the pressure.

This was the penultimate board:

Dealer South. Both vul.

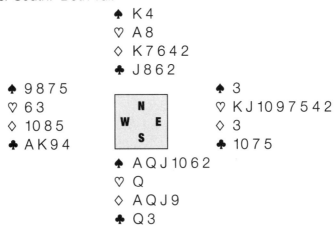

```
                    ♠ K 4
                    ♡ A 8
                    ◇ K 7 6 4 2
                    ♣ J 8 6 2
  ♠ 9 8 7 5                        ♠ 3
  ♡ 6 3              N             ♡ K J 10 9 7 5 4 2
  ◇ 10 8 5        W     E          ◇ 3
  ♣ A K 9 4          S             ♣ 10 7 5
                    ♠ A Q J 10 6 2
                    ♡ Q
                    ◇ A Q J 9
                    ♣ Q 3
```

Auntie Em opened the South hand One Spade and splintered in hearts over Hickory's Two Diamond response. The Tin Man had made a tactical decision to pass. Being vulnerable, and with the opposition already having bid spades, he felt that entering the auction would only be dangerous with the Scarecrow opposite.

Hickory quickly arrived in Six Diamonds, and the Scarecrow found himself in the passout seat looking at the ♣AK. Very mindful of his failure to double earlier, he cautiously pulled the red card out of his bidding tray, and this ended the auction.

The full auction had been:

West	North	East	South
Scarecrow	*Hickory*	*Tin Man*	*Auntie Em*
			1♠
pass	2◇	pass	3♡
pass	4NT	pass	5♡
pass	6◇	pass	pass
dbl	all pass		

The Tin Man mentally scratched his head. If the Scarecrow was doubling on two aces, then the lead probably didn't matter. Without the double, a club would have been the obvious lead.

The double, however, should be asking for him to do something different, such as leading dummy's suit. With Dorothy's pre-match advice about preserving partnership harmony in mind, as if he ever did anything else, he led the ♠3. Hickory won this in hand, played one round of diamonds to confirm they weren't 4-0, and claimed all thirteen tricks by discarding all four clubs in his hand on dummy's spades.

"Score is 1740, I think," said Auntie Em briskly as she put the final board on the table. Obviously, the last hand was now a formality. It wasn't clear, however, when they would be able to begin it. The Tin Man was taking some time delivering part two of his lecture, explaining the differences between doubling when on lead oneself, and doubling when trying to direct partner to the right start. The explanation was interspersed with a few words of encouragement, such as "cretin" and "moron," and Auntie Em was quite happy to let the Tin Man finish. The Scarecrow was quivering.

At the other table, the match had been going very much as Auntie Em had anticipated. They had in fact gained the expected 6 IMPs on the previous six boards but would discover, somewhat disappointingly, only a further 7 IMPs on this board, where after a heart preempt by East, Dorothy (South) ended up as declarer in Six Spades undoubled. On the lead of a top club, Dorothy had dropped the ♣Q, inducing a switch from Zeke. And so the final board appeared with Auntie Em's team leading by 18 IMPs.

The Scarecrow had taken charge of the boards to take his mind off other things and had rather muddled them up. The Tin Man could not hold back a snort when the board hit the table.

"Saving up all Em's boards for the end, I see," he commented, noting that South was dealer for the second board in a row.

Sitting in the West seat in each room, the Scarecrow and Zeke both looked at this hand:

♠ 10 9 7 3   ♡ A K 10 4   ◇ A 10 4 2   ♣ 8

Their right-hand opponents in the South seat, Auntie Em and Dorothy, respectively, opened One Club. Zeke, having had a good second set, had by now forgotten Auntie Em's strictures on his underbidding and, unnerved after his error on the previous board, considered a mere 11-count a clear pass. The Scarecrow, reduced to sheer instinct, didn't even stop to count his points, but seeing a suitable shape for a takeout double, acted on it.

The sequences at the two tables then proceeded as follows:

West	North	East	South
Scarecrow	*Hickory*	*Tin Man*	*Auntie Em*
			1♣
dbl	1♠	pass	2♣
pass	2◊	pass	3♣
pass	3♡	pass	3NT
pass	pass	dbl	all pass

West	North	East	South
Zeke	*Lion*	*Uncle H*	*Dorothy*
			1♣
pass	1♠	pass	2♣
pass	2◊	pass	2NT
pass	3NT	all pass	

The full hand was:

Dealer South. N/S vul.

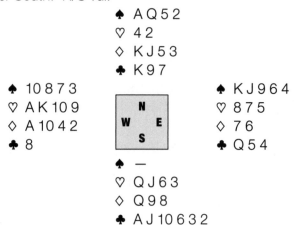

The Tin Man, having heard his partner's initial double, uttered a silent prayer that the Scarecrow might remember his most recent instructions and doubled the final contract for a spade lead.

In the other room, despite her rather unsuitable minimum, Dorothy reached the same contract by a faster route, afraid that the Lion might pass a Three Club bid, and eager to try for a vulnerable game to make up for what she feared might be happening in the other room.

On lead against Dorothy, Zeke chose the ♡A, seeking an attitude signal from Uncle Henry. When his partner discouraged the suit, he tried the ◊2 at the second trick. Dorothy won this in hand and knocked out the ◊A. Belatedly, Zeke tried a spade. Dorothy put in dummy's queen and won the next round with the ace in dummy.

By now it was clear to her that Zeke was short in clubs. She took the finesse and ten tricks were hers: six in clubs, one in spades and three in diamonds.

Events took a very different course in the other room. The Scarecrow's hands were like jelly as he fingered every card in his hand. Just as he was about to lead the ♡A, he looked at partner and trembled. He jumped. Oh yes, of course, he thought, the double was for a lead. What was it? He asked for a review of the bidding, given in exasperated tones by Auntie Em. Yes, it was dummy's first suit. He pulled out the ♠3.

Auntie Em looked at dummy with some distaste. She played the ♠5 and the Tin Man won the trick with his jack. A heart was returned, the Scarecrow beating Auntie Em's jack with his king, and this was followed by another spade to dummy's queen and the Tin Man's king. The Tin Man now played a heart to Auntie Em's queen and the Scarecrow's ace, and, not realizing at this point that the ♡109 were winners, he immediately returned the ♠10.

In desperation, Auntie Em won the trick and laid down the ♣K. It looked to her as if the Scarecrow had started with four cards in hearts and three in spades. It was likely he had a doubleton club. When she failed to drop the queen, she played a diamond, but the Scarecrow, desperate to lead his last spade, hopped up with the ace, and by the time the dust had cleared, Auntie Em had won only three tricks: her two aces and the ♣K.

"Score is 1400, I think," said the Tin Man, echoing Auntie Em's tone when she'd announced the result of the preceding hand. The Scarecrow automatically put this in the minus column of his spreadsheet. He had seen this score on a number of occasions, but had never before inscribed it on the plus side.

The Tin Man and the Scarecrow joined Dorothy outside. She called the Lion over: he had been explaining some of his courageously sound bids to Glinda. After scoring, adding up, and rechecking, the Lion was jubilant. The final board had brought in 19 IMPs, giving them victory by 1 IMP.

Dorothy congratulated the Scarecrow. "It was your double that did it," she said, "and then your lead." The Scarecrow listened uncomprehendingly. He had done something clever. And with the Tin Man as his partner! He even thought he had heard the Tin Man say, "Well done, partner," although he couldn't be sure that his ears hadn't been deceiving him.

Zeke, Hickory and Uncle Henry came in to congratulate them. Auntie Em remained frozen in her chair.

"Well done," said Uncle Henry graciously.

"Indeed," said Hickory. "We'll try to get revenge next year."

The Tin Man and the Scarecrow both turned pale. They had won the event. That meant they would have to defend it next year.

12

The Man Who Knew Too Much

"An orange juice, thank you," the Tin Man intoned, his full attention on the dummy in front of him.

"A glass of red wine," said the Lion. "A large one, if you don't mind," he added as an afterthought.

Dorothy went off to the bar. It was clear that the Lion needed sustenance. She had arrived while the last round was being played. Work had taken her to a meeting in Emerald City, and she had returned in time to join her friends for the post-mortem.

The Tin Man had not been pleased she had gone. "Surely you can tell them that you have a regular game on a Wednesday evening?" He never quite understood that Dorothy had an onerous job and that bridge could not always be given priority. "If you finish the meeting by three o'clock, you could probably still get here in time, or if they arranged it for Friday, then you could stay overnight, since we're playing there in the Swiss Teams on the weekend."

It was just a regular night at the Over the Rainbow Bridge Club, but one that saw some irregular partnerships. As well as Dorothy's absence, the Scarecrow had thought that he was going to be busy.

"Being restuffed, I imagine," joked the Tin Man as he arranged to play with the Lion.

Late in the day, the Scarecrow's appointment fell through and, with the Lion fixed up and Hank the Hunk grounded by Auntie Em for passing a cuebid, he hastily arranged to play with a Munchkin so shy that no one actually knew his name.

As the session ended, the Tin Man, the Lion, the Scarecrow, and Shy the Munchkin all meandered over to the club bar. Dorothy had bought the drinks and managed to hold a table for the five of them.

Shy wasn't much of a talker. That didn't bother the Tin Man, who felt that in conversation, as with declaring, he was entitled to an above average share. The others would be sure to want to hear about clever plays, which really meant he had to hold the floor.

There was one hand in particular that the Tin Man wanted to show to Dorothy.

Dealer North. N/S vul.

```
              ♠ 10 9 7 5 3
              ♡ 8 7
              ◇ A K J
              ♣ A K J
   ♠ K Q 6 4              ♠ A J 8 2
   ♡ K 5 4 3 2            ♡ 6
   ◇ 8 3         N        ◇ Q 10 7 6
   ♣ 4 3      W   E       ♣ Q 10 8 2
                 S
              ♠ —
              ♡ A Q J 10 9
              ◇ 9 5 4 2
              ♣ 9 7 6 5
```

The Lion opened the North hand a strong notrump. Reluctant as he was to put his hand down as dummy, the Tin Man seemed to have little choice but to transfer to hearts and hope for the best. The Lion bid Two Hearts, and that ended the auction:

West	North	East	South
	Lion		Tin Man
	1NT	pass	2◇*
pass	2♡	all pass	

East led the ♡6. The Lion, declarer as North, considered the situation. If everything lay exceptionally well, he could actually come to all thirteen tricks, but it was likely that he would have to lose a few along the way. Would people be in game? Probably not, he thought, with only 23 points and merely a seven-card heart fit. In any case, he would do his best to maximize his overtricks. He started by finessing the heart and was pleased when it won.

In no rush to repeat the finesse, he decided to take advantage of being in the dummy to take a finesse in one of the minor suits. He chose the club suit, and his jack lost to the queen. East returned a club, putting him in hand.

Playing his remaining heart, he got a shock when East showed out. After a pause, the Lion went up with the ace. His mood of optimism had vanished. Counting his tricks more carefully, he found that he would make four trump tricks, and then should probably win the ◊AK and, with luck, the ♣AK. He still had extra chances in both minors, but his only entries to hand were his trumps, and every time he ruffed something, he would be setting up a long trump for West. Playing on clubs was attractive. As long as West kept following, he would be taking tricks, and it would help him to know how many diamond tricks he needed.

Unfortunately, the third round of clubs was ruffed, leaving this position:

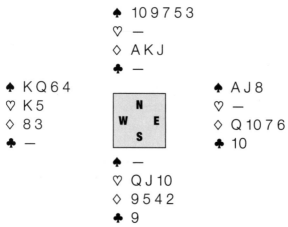

West played a diamond through and the Lion took what seemed to be his last chance for eight tricks by finessing the jack. However, East won and played the winning ♣10. He followed suit, and West discarded his remaining diamond. West now ruffed the diamond switch, cashed the ♡K, and then played the ♠K. The Lion still had a diamond loser. In total, he had managed to scrape together four trump tricks and the two minor-suit aces.

The Lion remembered only too well how he had felt at the table. "Bravo, bravo!" the Tin Man had cried. "Seldom have I seen so much good quality wine turned into rancid vinegar! To go two down with eight unbeatable tricks is a truly heroic performance! How inventive of you to find these extra losers."

While he was ranting, the Tin Man entered the score for the board. Suddenly he stopped. "Would you believe that someone outplayed you by four tricks? Yes, Four Hearts bid and made. What nonsense! I sometimes don't know why I bother." As he brought the next board onto the table, the Tin Man shook his head, while the Lion wished he had the Scarecrow opposite. The Scarecrow would never have commented, but that was because he would never have realized more tricks were available.

Shy and the Scarecrow had been listening to this. Shy nudged his partner and pointed to their scorecard, trying to indicate with his head that he should show it to the Tin Man. The Scarecrow looked confused, but Dorothy understood and asked if she could have a look.

"I think we have found out who made ten tricks," she said. "Tell us how you did it, Scarecrow." All eyes were on the Scarecrow.

They had played the hand against Ada and Cissie, two ladies who had been leading lights in the former women's club, the Lullaby League. The Scarecrow had felt relaxed as he sat down at their table. There was something almost Zen-like in playing with a partner who never once commented on any aspect of his bidding, play, or defense. All he got by way of feedback was a smile at the end of every hand.

"No Lion tonight?" Ada had asked the Scarecrow. "He's such a nice player, and a real gentleman."

"That he is," Cissie had agreed, cradling her handbag in her lap fondly. "Oh, but I see him over there playing with that crotchety Tin Man. Very kind of the Lion to give him a game, I would say."

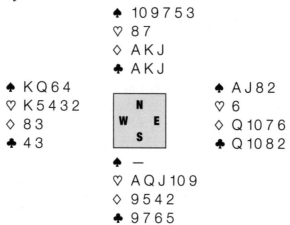

```
                  ♠ 10 9 7 5 3
                  ♡ 8 7
                  ◇ A K J
                  ♣ A K J
  ♠ K Q 6 4                        ♠ A J 8 2
  ♡ K 5 4 3 2          N           ♡ 6
  ◇ 8 3          W         E       ◇ Q 10 7 6
  ♣ 4 3                  S         ♣ Q 10 8 2
                  ♠ —
                  ♡ A Q J 10 9
                  ◇ 9 5 4 2
                  ♣ 9 7 6 5
```

The Scarecrow had experienced great difficulty in sorting out a system with Shy, who had simply nodded agreement to all of his suggestions, including both strong and weak notrumps. As a result, neither was entirely sure what values the other was showing in an auction that went as follows, with the Scarecrow occupying the South seat:

West	North	East	South
Ada	Shy	Cissie	Scarecrow
	1♠	pass	2♡
pass	2NT	pass	3♡
pass	4♡	all pass	

Ada, as West, led the ♠K and Shy smiled apologetically as he laid his hand down. The Scarecrow examined it with some dismay — being forced to ruff at Trick 1 was clearly not good and he had not had a lot of success with finesses recently. He decided to try to avoid going down until as late in the hand as possible.

The Scarecrow won the first trick by ruffing with the ♡9. Scorning any risky finesses, he crossed to the ♣A and ruffed another spade, then went back over to the ♣K, and ruffed a third spade. He repeated the same procedure in diamonds, entering dummy to ruff the fourth and fifth rounds of spades. His final spade ruff was with the ♡A, which West had to underruff holding nothing but trumps. Five ruffs and four minor-suit top cards had brought him to nine tricks and he had completed a most unlikely dummy reversal, leaving the following cards:

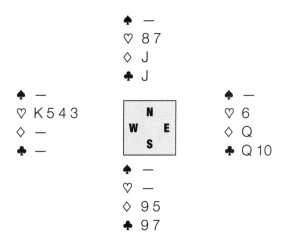

Dummy's hearts were of sufficient strength that he could not be prevented from scoring a tenth trick.

"Well played, indeed," said Ada, in the West seat. "You can imagine, Cissie, I thought about doubling."

"Very wise not to, Ada," Cissie replied. "They say that doubling usually costs a trick by giving away the position, and minus 790 would have been a real horror!" She shuddered visibly at the thought.

As the Scarecrow recounted these events, the Tin Man began to let out a low, involuntary hiss, signifying a mix of incredulity and a sneaking suspicion that the Scarecrow had stumbled onto a remarkably sensible line.

"Well done," said Dorothy, smiling at the Scarecrow. "You really did well on that one, and thoroughly earned your top."

The Scarecrow blushed.

The Tin Man's kettle appeared to have gone off the boil. He didn't appreciate others coming up with a better line than he had thought of. Rapidly, he moved the conversation onto a different board.

"You might find this instructive," he said, searching for it in the hand records. "I'm not sure which board it was, but here are our hands. I was in the South seat at this table." He found a napkin and set out the two hands:

♠ 10 8 5 4
♡ A K J 9 5
◇ 8
♣ J 8 3

♠ A K 7 6 2
♡ 6 3 2
◇ 3
♣ K Q 10 4

"With both sides vulnerable, our bidding was straightforward. When East opened One Diamond, I made the obvious overcall of One Spade. My partner was a passed hand, so his Three Heart bid over West's Three Diamonds had to show tricks in hearts and spade support. Knowing I was going to be at the helm, I had a clear-cut raise to game."

The full auction had been:

West	North	East	South
Munchkin	*Lion*	*Munchkin*	*Tin Man*
	pass	1◇	1♠
3◇	3♡	pass	4♠
all pass			

The Tin Man described the play. "West led the king of diamonds, placing him with the queen, and East played low to suggest a club switch. West played the seven of clubs to East's ace and another club came back, which I won in the dummy, West following with the two. I cashed the ace and king of spades, and found that West had started with three trumps headed by the jack, and East with the singleton queen. So, with two tricks lost and a certain trump loser, I had to avoid a heart loser."

He paused to ensure that everyone had time to assimilate the situation and appreciate the quality of his subsequent play. "There were, of course, two possibilities," he droned on. "One was to take a finesse and one was to play for the drop. East had shown one spade and either two or four clubs. His diamond length was unclear but probably five or six. East-West had not bid as much as one might expect with an eleven-card fit. Non-experts playing short minors often have problems with hands such as this. So, East seemed likely to hold between two and four hearts. In terms of points, he had shown two aces and a singleton jack. He could also have had the jack of diamonds, but all in all, it seemed quite likely that he had the queen of hearts.

"What about West?" continued the Tin Man. "Well, he had three spades, two or four clubs and again five or six diamonds. He was therefore likely to have one to three hearts. He had shown up with the king and queen of diamonds and the queen of spades. He might have had the queen of hearts, but did not need it for his bidding. Indeed, it could make his hand too strong for his jump to Three Diamonds. With that hand, I would have expected him to cuebid Two Spades.

"So, having concluded that East had the vital queen of hearts, I now played to make the contract." He paused again and looked meaningfully at his four companions: "Whether it dropped or not."

With a look of impending triumph on his face, the Tin Man came to the climax of his peroration. "The point to understand is that if East has queen doubleton, then it will fall under the ace-king, but if he has three to the queen, then West will have no hearts left and can be endplayed, if his exit cards are removed!

"My next step was therefore to cash the top hearts, on which both followed small. I then played out my club winners — if West ruffed in, he would have nothing but diamonds left and be forced to give me a ruff and discard. He didn't. Instead, he pitched a couple of diamonds, but to no avail, as I now put him in with the master trump, and on his forced diamond return, I ruffed in dummy and discarded my last heart." The Tin Man sat back and waited for their approbation.

The Scarecrow looked puzzled. "Well, actually, this was the last board we played. Shy was South on this hand. We also bid game and he made an overtrick. One other declarer also made eleven tricks on the hand.

"The lead was the seven of clubs to East's ace. Shy won the club return and took out two rounds of trumps. But the hand must have been misboarded, as he took the heart finesse and then was able to discard his diamond loser on the fourth heart. As West followed to three rounds of hearts he couldn't ruff in.

"You will get about an average, though," he said to comfort the Tin Man. "At a couple of tables, East-West sacrificed in Five Diamonds, and this went only two off for 500, compared to your 620." The Tin Man didn't seem at all comforted: averages were not things of glory for him.

The Lion had found the hand on the sheet. There had been no misboarding.

Dealer North. All vul.

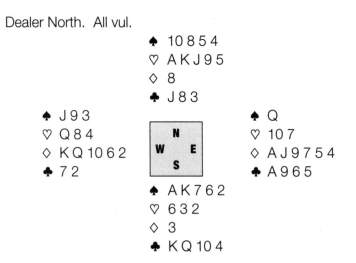

```
                    ♠ 10 8 5 4
                    ♡ A K J 9 5
                    ◇ 8
                    ♣ J 8 3
   ♠ J 9 3                           ♠ Q
   ♡ Q 8 4          N                ♡ 10 7
   ◇ K Q 10 6 2   W   E              ◇ A J 9 7 5 4
   ♣ 7 2            S                ♣ A 9 6 5
                    ♠ A K 7 6 2
                    ♡ 6 3 2
                    ◇ 3
                    ♣ K Q 10 4
```

"I can see that West might have had a problem here," said the Lion, puffing his chest out. "He probably didn't realize that you had no diamonds left and might have been worried that you were ruffing the heart."

"Not insightful defense, but not totally stupid," Dorothy commented.

The Lion wasn't to be stopped. "You said there were two ways to play hearts for no loser but you found a third one — a misdefense," he purred. "West must have read your mind and realized that he couldn't actually have the queen. How inventive of you to create an extra loser. A bit lucky, though, or you would have been the only person to go down! Still, better lucky than good."

13

Follow the Yellow Brick Road

"Welcome to Emerald City — the Nation's Jewel." The Tin Man snorted with derision at the sign as they entered the country's capital. "Typical! See themselves as the center of the universe! They see nothing of value outside their own little concrete square."

Dorothy's eyes were caught by a billboard that promised to dye your eyes to match your gown and decided not to bring it to his attention.

"And that idiot in the toll booth was so rude, so self-important," the Tin Man went on, oblivious of any part he might have had in riling said man. Dorothy squirmed with embarrassment as she remembered how they had nearly ended up missing the Swiss Teams with the Tin Man close to spending a night in a local cell.

"Well, I'm looking forward to having a game against some really good players," said Dorothy. "You know how stale we get playing against the same people every week."

"Indeed! And I enjoy that aspect of this sort of trip. In fairness, the good players are normally pleasant enough. It's the bumptious, distinctly average players who look down their noses at us just because we come from out of town that I can't stand."

"Well, the better we do, the more good players we will get to play."

"I hope so, though I'm not convinced about our team." This last was said in an undertone. Dorothy and the Tin Man were in the back seat of the Lion's large, gold car and the Lion and Dorothy's Uncle Henry were in the front.

"Surely you are relieved that the Scarecrow isn't playing?"

"Anyone, even your Uncle Henry, must be an improvement. Anyway, the Scarecrow is playing, just not in our team," corrected the Tin Man. "I have no doubt that he will be able to wreak some catastrophe upon us from the other side of the room."

It had come as a complete surprise to the Scarecrow to find a letter waiting for him at the club some weeks earlier. It was from a player he had met only once before. He was an Australian who had dropped into the club one night while on business in the town. He'd found the Scarecrow unpartnered for that evening and taken him to his highest-ever score before departing. The Scarecrow thought that the visitor was probably quite a good player, but attributed their success to the way he had been able to bring out the best in the Australian.

It transpired that the Australian was going to be in the country at the time of the Emerald City Swiss Teams and had written inviting the Scarecrow to play with him in it. The Australian had suggested that they team up with two friends of his, Jack and Ken, local players from Emerald City. He omitted to tell the Scarecrow that the pair had played in fourteen international matches for their country. However, he had warned Jack and Ken that he and the Scarecrow might come back with some surprising scores. He had told them that he wanted to play with a partner who would in all likelihood produce some quite remarkable results, not all of a positive nature, and asked if they were willing to be teammates. Slightly mystified, they had agreed.

Uncle Henry had heard that Dorothy's team was a player short and had approached the Lion, whom he felt was solid and straightforward enough to match his style. The Lion accepted readily. Uncle Henry was not the sort of player to overbid wildly, and, like almost every other member of the club, would be an improvement on the Scarecrow.

The Scarecrow had arrived in Emerald City the day before and had suggested a practice session at a local club. The Australian had politely declined, suggesting instead a meal and a bottle of wine at their hotel. The time had seemed to pass very rapidly, the Scarecrow thought, as the elevator took him up to his third-floor bedroom. He had intended to discuss some system ideas but realized with surprise that they hadn't discussed any system issues whatsoever. Instead, the Australian had shown great interest in the Over the Rainbow Bridge Club and seemed particularly interested in the Great Air Conditioning Affair and other similar witch-related controversies.

The random draw for the first round had set the Australian's team against a sound local team. In a very dull set of eight boards, they scored six VPs out of a possible twenty. There were a few single IMPs coming in, but the Scarecrow had passed a cuebid in a successful attempt to avoid playing a hand. Sadly, despite the Australian's prowess as declarer, he had been unable to magic up many tricks in the 3-0 fit, and a game swing against, fortunately non-vulnerable, was the result. However, his partner and teammates were so nice about it that the Scarecrow felt perfectly calm going into the second round.

The Scarecrow had never seen so many tables in play at one time. In round two, they took the North-South seats at table 87, still 41 tables away from the bottom of the field.

"Hey, it's the card wizard!" The approaching East-West pair clearly knew the Australian well. He introduced them as Ray and Arthur. Once again, he omitted to perturb his partner with the information that both opponents had a string of trophies to their names.

"Are you playing with John and George?" he asked them.

"No, George is on holiday — most inconsiderate of him. John is playing with George's other partner, Paul."

"If only George was here, and they could find a Ringo, what a team that would be!" joked the Australian.

On the critical board of the match, John and Paul were not in harmony.

Dealer South. Both vul.

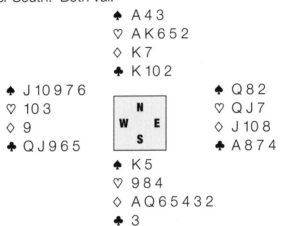

West	North	East	South
Ken	John	Jack	Paul
			1◇
pass	1♡	pass	2♡
pass	2NT	pass	3◇
pass	3♡	all pass	

When Paul, South, passed Three Hearts, a look of incredulity passed over John's face. "Surely we both play Two Notrump as a game-forcing relay when we play with George?"

"I do, but I didn't know that you did, so I assumed that it was just some sort of game try." He tabled dummy.

John cursed under his breath. "We can only hope that they get overboard and bid a slam." He quickly wrapped up eleven tricks for the loss of the ♣A and a trump.

The auction was shorter at the other table.

West	North	East	South
Ray	Australian	Arthur	Scarecrow
			3◊
pass	6◊	all pass	

The Australian had found that, playing with the Scarecrow, the longer the auction, the more scope for a disaster. One of the few agreements that he and the Scarecrow had made was that vulnerable preempts would show at least two of the top three honors. The Australian had every hope that slam would be playable, preferably laydown.

West led the ♣Q, which was ducked all around, and then switched to the ♠J, won by the Scarecrow's king. Declarer played four rounds of trumps. The extra round saved the tedious exertion of counting, and experience had shown him how often an extra little trump could be left lurking about. He then played a spade to the ace and ruffed dummy last spade.

Though it may not have been obvious, the Scarecrow had formed a plan. Well, a strategy might have been a better word for it. He had been able to spot eleven tricks and had calculated that one more would bring the contract home. His best hope seemed to be the ♣K, so he was keeping an eye out in case someone mistakenly discarded the ♣A. His second string was his heart suit. Sometimes, surprising small cards could turn into winners, and on this occasion he had mild aspirations for the ♡9. As a result, he was keeping half an eye out for heart discards, preferably honors. He was aware that these two tasks required significant mental energy and fully justified sacrificing lesser matters, like counting trumps.

After eight tricks he paused briefly to take stock. They were down to:

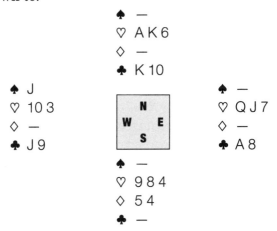

```
                    ♠ —
                    ♡ A K 6
                    ◊ —
                    ♣ K 10
   ♠ J                              ♠ —
   ♡ 10 3          ┌─────────┐      ♡ Q J 7
   ◊ —             │    N    │      ◊ —
   ♣ J 9           │  W   E  │      ♣ A 8
                   │    S    │
                   └─────────┘
                    ♠ —
                    ♡ 9 8 4
                    ◊ 5 4
                    ♣ —
```

The Scarecrow was fairly sure that no one had thrown the ♣A. Indeed, he would feel disappointed if he had missed that. He had seen two hearts go. No, hang on, he had thrown them from the dummy. He thought he would try one more trump. He played the ◊5.

West pitched the ♠J, dummy parted with the ♡6, and East found that he had run out of safe discards. Throwing a club would allow declarer to enter dummy with a heart and ruff out the ♣A. He pitched a heart instead.

The Scarecrow was getting excited. He now played his last trump, the ◊4. West followed with the ♡3, and it was at this point that the Scarecrow noticed something odd. His card and East's card had more in common than their color. He realized he had played the wrong red four.

He won in the dummy and for the lack of anything better to do, played the other top heart. Still no one had discarded the ♣A, so he led the ♣10, ruffed it, and conceded the last heart. He looked puzzled when the opponents swept up their cards and returned them to board.

"Very well played," said Arthur. "So rare to see someone play a trump squeeze so effortlessly. You must have seen the position very early."

The Scarecrow blushed, confused. "Well, you know, sometimes these hands just play themselves," he mumbled.

"Indeed," Arthur continued. "But only if you have mastered the technique. As I said, well done."

Turning to the Australian, Ray commented, "Perhaps we should all take a leaf out of your book and look for talent outside of the city."

The Australian beamed. "Not only talented, but a sheer pleasure to play with, I can assure you."

A win in this match combined with another in the third round took the Australian's team to 40 VPs out of a possible 60, and they rose to Table 25. As fate would have it, this brought them up against Dorothy's team, which had edged up the field with three 13-7 wins.

The Lion was walking proudly up and down the gap between the second and third rows, hoping to be seen, looking for anyone to ask how his team was faring, so he could answer nonchalantly, "Oh, you know, unbeaten so far." The Tin Man was relatively placid. He found scoring up with the Lion and Henry less frustrating than when the Scarecrow was involved, though he still felt that they ought to be at least 10 VPs better off, and that the missed opportunities were not at his table.

The third board of the next round seemed to offer lots of opportunities for a swing.

Dealer West. N/S vul.

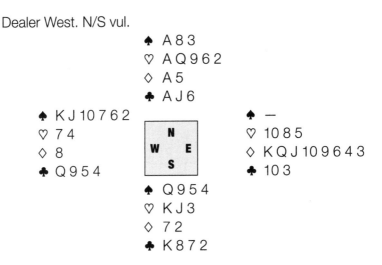

<pre>
              ♠ A 8 3
              ♡ A Q 9 6 2
              ◇ A 5
              ♣ A J 6
♠ K J 10 7 6 2   ♠ —
♡ 7 4   N   ♡ 10 8 5
◇ 8   W   E   ◇ K Q J 10 9 6 4 3
♣ Q 9 5 4   S   ♣ 10 3
              ♠ Q 9 5 4
              ♡ K J 3
              ◇ 7 2
              ♣ K 8 7 2
</pre>

Ken, in the West seat, opened a weak Two Spades, and the Tin Man had to decide how best to develop the auction with his 19-count. He felt his hand was too good for an immediate Three Hearts, so he doubled. Jack, as East, had a classic preemptive hand, and the vulnerability in his favor, so he applied maximum pressure on the opposition with an overcall of Five Diamonds. Dorothy was too strong to pass, so tried to give her partner some idea of her hand by doubling. The Tin Man was torn between taking the money and going for the vulnerable game bonus. The lure of the unbid five-card major was too much and he pulled to Five Hearts.

West	North	East	South
Ken	*Tin Man*	*Jack*	*Dorothy*
2♠	dbl	5◇	dbl
pass	5♡	all pass	

Jack led the ◇K. The Tin Man was not best pleased by dummy. It might have been fairer to criticize himself for his failure to pass, but it was more satisfying to blame his partner. He won the ◇A and played a heart to dummy's king. After cashing the

♡J, he finessed the ♣J, then drew the remaining trump, West discarding a spade. The ♣A and a further club to dummy's king revealed the 4-2 split. They were down to:

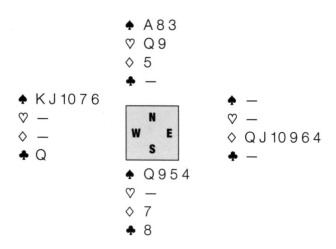

With the lead in dummy in the South hand, the Tin Man had ten tricks assured and needed to find one more. The hand was an open book to the Tin Man. He called for dummy's last club and pitched his losing diamond on it. West had to lead away from his spades, giving declarer the extra trick he needed.

"Well done," said Dorothy.

"Looks like my Five Diamonds was going for 800," said Jack. "Perhaps it was a bit pushy on my part."

"Seems like a normal bid," Ken replied, taking Jack's hand out of the board. "Worth the gamble of losing 4 IMPs to put them under pressure."

Events took a very different turn at the other table. The Lion and Uncle Henry had agreed to play a Multi Two Diamonds. Henry was glad of the chance, because Auntie Em refused to countenance anything so artificial and then always told people that he was the one who refused to try things out. The Lion had always feared that in the Scarecrow's hands the Multi would be a weapon of mutually assured destruction. This seemed like a safer time to give it a go.

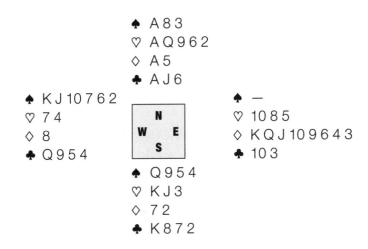

```
                    ♠ A 8 3
                    ♡ A Q 9 6 2
                    ◇ A 5
                    ♣ A J 6
  ♠ K J 10 7 6 2                         ♠ —
  ♡ 7 4              ┌─────────┐         ♡ 10 8 5
  ◇ 8               │    N    │          ◇ K Q J 10 9 6 4 3
  ♣ Q 9 5 4        │  W   E  │          ♣ 10 3
                    │    S    │
                    └─────────┘
                    ♠ Q 9 5 4
                    ♡ K J 3
                    ◇ 7 2
                    ♣ K 8 7 2
```

The Lion opened Two Diamonds and the Scarecrow doubled,
an undiscussed call that his partner rightly took as meaning
that he had a good hand and didn't know what to do. Henry
puzzled over his hand. If his partner's suit was hearts, then
his hand was huge, but if it was spades, then it fitted less well.
He bid Three Diamonds. The Australian decided that there
was no safe way of entering the auction so he passed, as did
the Lion. The Scarecrow still had a good hand and still did not
know what to do, so he doubled again. As Uncle Henry edged
forward with Four Diamonds, the Lion shifted nervously in
his seat. The Australian felt he had too much strength to pass
again. Not unaware of the advantages of declaring the contract
himself, he chanced his arm with Four Spades.

The Lion tried to calm himself. Just a few seconds ago,
he had visions of a catastrophic end to this auction. Now he
reflected that it was for moments like this that people played
the Multi. Could the opponents run to a better spot? Surely
not. Very delicately, he pulled a double from his box and put
it down on the table. After two slow passes and a slight shrug
from the Australian, the Lion led his singleton diamond.

West	North	East	South
Lion	*Scarecrow*	*Uncle H*	*Australian*
2◊	dbl	3◊	pass
pass	dbl	4◊	4♠
dbl	all pass		

It was immediately clear to the Australian that he was playing in the Lion's suit, and that he would have to restrict his outside losers to a minimum. He won the ◊A, played a heart to hand, and led a trump towards the dummy. The Lion put the ten in and the Australian took the ace. He played another heart to hand and then successfully finessed the ♣J. The ♣A and ♣K followed. The suit didn't split, but he was able to ruff the fourth round of the suit in dummy. With eight tricks taken by declarer, and none lost, the players were down to:

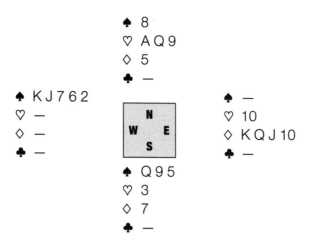

Declarer led the ♡A from dummy, which the Lion ruffed. A high or low spade was going to be immediately fatal, so he led the ♣J. The Australian won the queen and put the Lion back on lead by playing his diamond. The Lion now held ♠K7 over the Australian's ♠95 and could not avoid giving declarer a tenth trick: +790.

They went back to their teammates' table to score up. When they got to this board, the Tin Man called out, "Plus 650."

"Lose four," said the Lion.

"What happened?" asked the Tin Man.

"We went for 800 in Five Diamonds," said the Lion, standing on Henry's foot when he was about to protest.

"Hmm, yes, reasonable," said the Tin Man.

The match turned out to be a tie, leaving both teams a bit above average with three rounds to go. The Lion was delighted that their unbeaten record was intact. Dorothy was relieved not to have lost to the Scarecrow. The Tin Man sensed the sands of time slipping away — they needed to step on the gas to get a good finish. Uncle Henry massaged his bunions.

The Sound of Silence

There was a sense of excitement in the air at the venue: the Emerald City Conference Center was accommodating 128 tables in its second biggest hall. Almost all the best players in the country were there, and after four of the seven matches, the leading score was 63 VPs out of a possible 80.

The Tin Man, Dorothy, the Lion and Dorothy's Uncle Henry were holding their own. Indeed, to the delight of three of them, they were unbeaten with a score of 49 VPs. The Tin Man took a rather different view.

"Fourteen VPs off the lead! We could so easily have been there! It's not the boards we've lost on; it's the opportunities we've missed. Take that good slam in the second match, or the Moysian heart game in the third match, or the Three Spades in the first match that could have been made on a simple squeeze. They may have been flat boards but — "

"Our time would be better spent congratulating ourselves on our good results against high-quality teams." Dorothy's interruption was in a tone that made it very clear that the discussion was closed. She could see the Lion squirming. There was one factor common to all three of the boards the Tin Man had referred to. The missed potential had occurred at the other table. Dorothy was fully aware that a similar list could have been produced for their table, but she also knew how hopeless it would be trying to get the Tin Man to see this. The most she could do was change the subject before team morale was completely destroyed.

It was now just after four o'clock on Sunday afternoon, and the event had a 90-minute meal break. Every year, the contestants complained about the break being at a time of the day when few places were serving food, but every year it remained the same. The Tin Man knew a café just five minutes away, which he always insisted on going to when playing bridge in the City. Describing it as a "greasy spoon" was probably being complimentary. Nevertheless, Dorothy was the only member of the team who was less than enamored with the place. The Lion was not too choosy when it came to food, and Uncle Henry relished the chance to tuck into some of the high-cholesterol delicacies that Auntie Em had put on his banned list.

The fifth member of the Over the Rainbow Bridge Club playing that day, the Scarecrow, was enjoying his time partnering the talented player from Australia. The Australian knew that his teammates' easy-going attitude would be an asset when scoring up, and they hadn't disappointed him. This team had reached 50 VPs by a path involving peaks and valleys, as opposed to the steady progress of the Tin Man's team.

At the meal break, Ken and Jack took their team to a Chinese restaurant they knew well, just a short drive away. The Scarecrow decided to take the buffet option, and found it hard to resist refilling his plate at least twice more than nutrition required. The effects were disastrous. Two hands into Round Five, his digestive system demanded that full power be diverted from his brain to his stomach. He failed to open the bidding on a 15-count and a slam was missed. Two boards later, he revoked, letting a game through, and then he forgot that they were playing the same notrump range as he did with the Lion, which led to another catastrophe. Being on the wrong end of a 20-0 score pulled them back to the middle of the field.

Dorothy's team, meanwhile, retained their unbeaten record, scoring another 12 VPs. The Tin Man was starting to become twitchy. For a place in the prizes, they needed a top-ten finish, meaning they would have to improve their scoring in the last two rounds.

He and Dorothy finished Round Six ahead of their teammates. They were hovering a couple of rows away from the Lion and Uncle Henry's table, at an island of tables that had completed the round. They were joined by the Scarecrow and his Australian partner, who were also waiting.

The Tin Man was nervously optimistic. He knew that their card was good, but it was not beyond the capacity of his teammates to blow it.

"What did you do on board fifteen?" he asked the Australian. Not waiting for an answer, he recounted the events at his table.

Dealer South. N/S vul.

```
                    ♠ —
                    ♡ A K J 5
                    ◇ A K 10 8 6 3
                    ♣ Q 8 5
      ♠ J 7                          ♠ K 10 9 8 4 3 2
      ♡ 6             ┌─────────┐    ♡ 9 8 2
      ◇ Q J 7 2       │    N    │    ◇ 4
      ♣ J 9 7 6 4 2   │ W     E │    ♣ K 10
                      │    S    │
                      └─────────┘
                    ♠ A Q 6 5
                    ♡ Q 10 7 4 3
                    ◇ 9 5
                    ♣ A 3
```

West	North	East	South
	Dorothy		Tin Man
			1♡
pass	2NT	4♠	dbl
pass	5♠	pass	5NT
pass	6♣	pass	6NT
pass	7♡	all pass	

"We had a routine auction," the Tin Man said with the tone of one who bids a good grand slam every few boards. "Two Notrump showed four-card support and was either game-forcing balanced or very strong unbalanced. Five Spades was clearly Exclusion Keycard, and Six Clubs showed one keycard outside spades. All Dorothy had to do was check I had the trump queen, which Six Notrump showed, and it was obvious to bid the grand. She had the added assurance of knowing I would be at the helm.

"West led the ♣6 and I viewed dummy with a certain degree of satisfaction," the Tin Man continued to his captive audience. "If trumps were 2-2, then I could afford to ruff diamonds twice. Even if they were 3-1, I still had excellent chances. It was irritating that West had had the sense not to lead a spade, but then, we didn't come this far to play against Munchkins!

"I called for the queen of clubs and took the king with my ace. Now I played a trump to dummy's ace and returned to hand with a second trump. It was obviously a disappointment to see West show out on this.

"I needed to develop diamond tricks to take care of my black losers, and I was about to draw a third trump and hope for diamonds to be 3-2 when I stopped myself." The Tin Man paused for effect to ensure that the brilliancy he was about to disclose was fully appreciated by all. "I could mentally write down at least seven spades in the East hand, and I knew for sure about three hearts. The king of clubs made eleven known cards. What were the other two? Two diamonds? No! That would have meant that West had led low from a suit headed by the jack-ten-nine! The ten of clubs had to be in the East hand so there was room for at most one diamond."

He glanced at the Australian to ensure he had his full attention. "Given that there were two high diamonds and three low ones outstanding," the Tin Man continued, "the odds were obviously in favor of the singleton being low. I led the nine of diamonds from hand and ran it. When that scored, I drew the last trump with the ten of hearts in my hand and played a second diamond. East put in the jack, but it was all over at this point. I took the ace-king (discarding my losing club), ruffed out the queen of diamonds, and reentered the North hand with a spade ruff. Dummy's diamonds allowed me to discard my two losing spades!" The Tin Man's lips curled upwards in what experts in the field recognized as his version of a smile.

"Well done," said the Australian. "Nice inference in clubs. I was in the heart grand slam, too. You'll never guess what lead I got: the jack of clubs!" He paused, while the Tin Man and Dorothy took in the implications.

"Fiendish!" said Dorothy. "You can't read the clubs now." The Tin Man looked perplexed, not wanting to commit himself.

The Australian let him off the hook. "I'm sure that you would get it right at the table. Would West have led away from a king against a grand slam? No. We can place the king in the East hand, and the way to find out if it is a singleton or not is to play low at Trick 1. If the king comes up, then you have no club loser, but if, as happened, the ten comes in, then you are back in the situation you described."

"Indeed so," said the Tin Man, trying to avoid looking deflated as this upstart Australian had found the same winning line as he had. Even worse, it had just occurred to him that it would have been an improvement on his line to play low from the dummy at Trick 1.

The Scarecrow's team had won 18-2 and jumped well up the field. The Tin Man's team had scored a 16-4 win, which took them up to ninth place, but his hopes of an easy draw for the last round evaporated when he saw four internationalists approaching. This team had played the Scarecrow's team in the second round. Dorothy and the Tin Man would be against Ray and Arthur, a partnership of many years standing. The Lion and Uncle Henry faced John and Paul — both excellent players but not a regular partnership. Thanks to their partner in common, a man called George, they had spent the day listening to variations on "Where's Ringo?" jokes. Fortunately for them, the Beatles were a little on the modern side for Uncle Henry, and the Lion was too much in awe of them to attempt any witticisms.

As Ray took his seat against Dorothy and the Tin Man, he commented, "I was told you're the regular teammates of the gentleman we met in round two. He handled that trump squeeze so effortlessly, and with your team up here in the top row, your bridge club must have a high standard." It took three boards before the Tin Man regained his composure.

Once again, the Tin Man and Dorothy finished quickly and found themselves waiting anxiously with the talented Australian and the Scarecrow. On the whole, the Tin Man estimated, the match had gone reasonably well. But there were two early hands on which he had gone down that were worrying him. Against Munchkins he would not have been concerned, but he feared that top-class players might have found a way of outperforming him.

This was the first one.

Dealer South. Both vul.

```
                    ♠ 3
                    ♡ J 8 7
                    ◇ K J 10 6 2
                    ♣ 10 6 3 2
  ♠ K 2                              ♠ 10 9 8 7
  ♡ Q 9 6 4 3                        ♡ A K
  ◇ 9 8                              ◇ 7 4 3
  ♣ J 9 8 4                          ♣ K Q 7 5
                    ♠ A Q J 6 5 4
                    ♡ 10 5 2
                    ◇ A Q 5
                    ♣ A
```

West	North	East	South
Ray	Dorothy	Arthur	Tin Man
			1♠
pass	1NT	pass	3♠
all pass			

Ray, West, led a Heart. Arthur, East, won and took his second top heart before switching to the ♣K. The Tin Man won perforce with his singleton ace. He could see four certain losers: three hearts and at least one trump. The Tin Man explained his thought process at this point to the Australian.

"If trumps were 4-2, then I was sunk unless I found East with the doubleton king. There was an additional risk in crossing to the dummy in diamonds and taking a losing trump finesse in that I might then run into a diamond ruff, but I decided that it was worth it. As you know, the finesse lost and trumps didn't break for me, so I went one down. I see that you made it on a heart lead."

"Yes," answered the Australian. "The play was the same for the first three tricks. Like you, I started thinking about the trump suit and the possibility of a diamond ruff. Then I realized that I was missing something much more devastating — a heart ruff."

The Tin Man narrowed his eyes. "Goodness, yes. Even if trumps break 3-3, then if the defense get in early in trumps, a fourth round of hearts will allow a trump promotion. Playing trumps from the top will never work unless the hand with the long hearts has no entry. Surely that is an argument in favor of my line?"

"Quite so," the Australian said, nodding, "but your line only worked for a doubleton king or Kxx with East. With hearts looking like they were 5-2, I figured that an even spade break was even less likely than the normal thirty-six percent, and with East having already shown up with a lot of points without entering the bidding, I felt that the finesse was likely to lose. I decided to take a line to cater for doubleton king in either hand and without the risk of a first- or second-round diamond ruff. I played the ace of spades and then a low one. Today I got lucky."

The Tin Man was impressed. "Well played," he said. "It is so rare to be able to talk with someone who genuinely thinks about a hand."

The Tin Man could live with the loss of a partscore swing, but was more concerned about a slam he had gone down in on the first board they had played in the match.

Dealer West. E/W vul.

```
                    ♠ A 10
                    ♡ 4
                    ◇ A Q 9 8 5
                    ♣ A K Q 8 5
  ♠ K J 7 6 5 3                      ♠ 2
  ♡ 5                 ┌─────────┐    ♡ J 10 7 6 2
  ◇ J 10 7 3 2       │    N    │    ◇ 6
  ♣ 10              │ W     E │    ♣ J 9 7 6 4 2
                     │    S    │
                     └─────────┘
                    ♠ Q 9 8 4
                    ♡ A K Q 9 8 3
                    ◇ K 4
                    ♣ 3
```

West	North	East	South
Ray	Dorothy	Arthur	Tin Man
2♠	3◇	pass	4♡
pass	4NT	pass	5♠
pass	6♡	all pass	

Dorothy did not especially like her Three Diamonds bid, but it seemed the best first move on the hand. When the Tin Man jumped to Four Hearts, she knew that he must have a very good suit, and she had controls aplenty in the other suits. The RKCB response reassured her that he held the top three hearts, but she felt it was asking too much to try a grand slam.

Ray, sitting West, led the ♣10 and the Tin Man won in the dummy. Things were looking good. If trumps were 3-3, then he was home with no problem. If they were 4-2, he would hope to be able to dispose of his spade losers on dummy's minors once three trumps had been drawn.

Again the Tin Man explained his thoughts to the Australian. "So I played two top trumps and then found out about the 5-1 break. It's a good slam, but extremely unlucky. I wonder if any slam can make. It looks like the bad breaks in every suit will stop Six Notrump unless there is a squeeze." He looked at the Australian's card. "What! You made Six Hearts? Surely East didn't split his top hearts?"

"No, indeed not. You are right, of course, about your prospects if trumps break reasonably, but what about if they are 5-1? If there are five on your left, which is extremely unlikely after the weak-two opening, then you have no chance. But what about five on the right? That gives West a singleton, and as you are missing four low hearts and two high ones, that makes the finesse a two-to-one favorite. If trumps are 4-2, then no harm has been done and if they are 3-3, then you may lose an overtrick. But then we aren't playing matchpoints. Of course, you can't take the trump finesse if you have a potential spade loser. Fortunately, the lead at our table was the ten of clubs."

The Tin Man's face went an extra shade of gray as he tried to remember if he had divulged that he had also received that lead. "Yes, you are right. That's two hands I've lost through not thinking fully about trump control." He glanced at the Australian's card. "So I assume that is how you made it. Well played again."

"Well, I hope I might have taken that line, but to be honest, I didn't play the hand. My partner, your friend the Scarecrow, had put the board on the table the wrong way, so he ended up playing the contract, and, yes, he played the finesse."

Dorothy gasped. "Are you saying he worked out a safety play like that?"

"Oh, I couldn't say. I doubt he knew at the time why he was doing it. I didn't ask him. I'm sure he couldn't tell us now. I have found him to be a most instinctive player, and when he follows his instincts it seems to work more in our favor than against us. Still, of all people, I don't need to tell you that!"

The Australian noticed that his teammates had finished play and went to score up with them. The Tin Man stood rooted to the spot.

Dorothy broke the silence. "He really is a bit of a wizard with the cards, that man from Oz. Anyway, the scores at his table don't matter to us. We'll just have to see what our men have been up to." As she finished speaking, she saw the Lion and Uncle Henry stand up and move away from their table. The Tin Man set off at pace to meet them and Dorothy caught them up just in time to score, thanks to a short delay while Uncle Henry searched for the glasses he had taken off thirty seconds earlier.

The scoring seemed to take an age. Uncle Henry couldn't always read his own writing, and the Lion had a number of scores in the wrong place. The Three Spades he had gone down in cost 4 IMPs when the opposition had the methods to stop at the two-level. There were a number of smaller swings and the Tin Man, who was keeping a running total in his head, knew that they were 1 IMP down with just the slam hand left to score.

"Minus 50," he muttered in resignation.

"Got a hundred," said the Lion.

"They weren't vulnerable," the Tin Man checked, as this had been a problem several times in the course of the day.

"Yes, they were — to us!" preened the Lion.

This is what had happened.

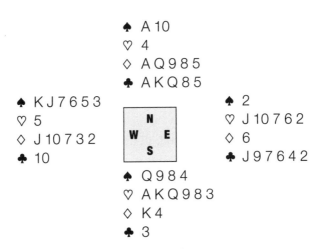

	♠ A 10	
	♡ 4	
	◊ A Q 9 8 5	
	♣ A K Q 8 5	
♠ K J 7 6 5 3		♠ 2
♡ 5		♡ J 10 7 6 2
◊ J 10 7 3 2		◊ 6
♣ 10		♣ J 9 7 6 4 2
	♠ Q 9 8 4	
	♡ A K Q 9 8 3	
	◊ K 4	
	♣ 3	

West	North	East	South
Uncle H	*John*	*Lion*	*Paul*
3♠	4NT	pass	5NT
pass	6♣	pass	6◊
pass	7◊	all pass	

Uncle Henry and the Lion were playing Multi, but following an early disaster with the convention, Uncle Henry had either upgraded or downgraded all his six-card majors. With the extra shape, he had decided that this was one to upgrade.

North-South came unstuck due to their lack of methods. Paul was not happy with dummy. "Surely that's a grand slam try? If you only had slam values and the red suits, you would jump to Six Diamonds over Four Notrump?"

"I thought we agreed that Five Notrump was pick-a-slam. I knew that you had the minors, but you could still have something in hearts. I was just trying to reach the best small slam."

"But when I bid Four Notrump, surely we can assume we are playing in one of my suits? It must be better to use this sort of sequence to decide what level we are playing at. I suppose we'll need to add this to the list of things to ask George about."

The Lion had led his spade. Paul could see that regardless of the misunderstanding, the contract was not hopeless. If the trumps and hearts broke, then he would get home. Sadly for him, it was not to be. Indeed, when he discovered the 5-1 trump break, he did extremely well, aided by less than incisive defense, to get out for two down.

The 1 IMP win gave them 11 VPs. They had to wait anxiously for the other matches to finish. It was worth the wait. A 19-1 win for the Scarecrow and team, largely due to his brilliantly played slam, propelled them up to tenth place, 1 VP behind the Tin Man, Dorothy, Uncle Henry, and the Lion.

The Lion was bursting with pride as he power-walked back from the recap sheet, his golden mane bouncing with each stride. Dorothy and her Uncle Henry felt pretty pleased with themselves. The Scarecrow had never imagined that he would be well placed and was beside himself with joy. He felt, in his modest way, that once again he had managed to bring out the best in this Wizard chap. The only person from the Over the Rainbow Bridge Club who left feeling subdued was the Tin Man. If there was anything more important to him than a high place, it was playing better than everyone else. On this day, and even into the early part of the following week, he found himself feeling unaccustomed humility.

Epilogue

The Honorary Chairman of the Lollipop Guild sighed and reached for his cocoa, only to find that, like his first cup, this one had gone cold, largely undrunk. He was a man of many hats: a member of various committees and, in his younger days, a politician. He was grateful that the job of herding the local council towards vaguely sensible decisions now fell to his long-time friend and bridge partner. Being Mayor of Munchkinland was a thankless task, but he could think of no better preparation for the far more difficult job of being president of the Over the Rainbow Bridge Club.

It had been a tradition for the President to write his annual Letter to Members for the November edition of the Club magazine, the last before Christmas. How should he sum up the year, and what message should he give them for the year ahead?

"It hardly seems like a year since I was last writing my annual address," he began, cutting and pasting from last year's text. That much was true. He leaned back in his chair and reflected. He was used to dealing with people. Well, normal people at least. But how much use was that when each member of the Club had his or her own peculiar view of the world and their importance in it?

Take Auntie Em, for example. Yes, she was supportive of his role and very active in developing every aspect of the club. But once she had an idea fixed in her mind, heaven help anyone who tried to resist. Older, long-departed members of the Club had told him that in his youth Uncle Henry had been an outgoing, spirited young man, full of fresh thinking. Now he wouldn't dare to voice any opinion until he'd been told what that opinion was!

Auntie Em had certainly done a lot for the Club. Some of her farmhands, carefully selected at the recruitment stage, had now developed into capable players. It was well known that Hank the Hunk had been hired while Auntie Em had been away visiting her sister in the Emerald City, and that Uncle Henry had never been forgiven for this serious oversight. But Auntie Em had a soft heart somewhere, well hidden within her, and Hank being so keen, she just couldn't bring herself to dismiss him.

The Chairman's thoughts turned to the winners of the Club's Perfect Teams. Perfect! How could any team containing that Scarecrow ever be called "perfect"? The Scarecrow's main contribution to the Club was that all its tournament directors were now experts on some of the most obscure situations in the rulebook. In the Scarecrow's hands, anything could go wrong, and everything usually did. Yet somehow, despite the laws being designed to penalize the offending player, he invariably seemed to come out of each drama he created smelling of roses!

How could a team with two perfectly reasonable members out of four, that is, the Lion and Dorothy, actually create so many problems for the Committee? Sorting out the chaos caused by the Scarecrow was a simple technical task compared to soothing the ruffled feelings of member after member in every session the Tin Man played. And he was the person tasked with reprimanding the Tin Man. It would have been easier to negotiate with Genghis Khan! The Tin Man would never understand the effect of what he said and did on the more sensitive souls in the Club.

There was a big difference, however, between the Tin Man and the witches. At least the Tin Man had no idea whatsoever of the carnage in his wake. But it could not be denied, much as the Chairman tried to look for the best in people, that the witches delighted in creating mayhem. Well, three of them anyway. His heart melted at the thought of the lovely Glinda, with her cascading blond hair. He laughed out loud at this one pleasant thought before memories of the antics of her three colleagues brought him back to reality with a shudder. He could not entirely dismiss the possibility that the awful flu epidemic last winter could be laid at the door of the Unpleasant Witch of the North. Certainly, she had been one of the first victims, and her contribution to the buffet at the Christmas party had been accompanied by helpings of sneezes and wheezes.

Yes, with members like these, the Over the Rainbow Bridge Club was truly like no other. Would things change? No, of course not. There would be much the same people in charge and much the same people winning the prizes. But *plus ça change, plus c'est la même chose.*

And yet there were bound to be surprises in store. Wars would no doubt be won and lost, new characters would make their presence felt, and old characters would not give up the limelight easily. The Chairman mused on his hopes for the year ahead. A peaceful year, and at least two complete tops against the Tin Man. He would have had one only last week if he'd been able to find the right switch at the critical moment in the play. "If you'd only had a heart..." the Tin Man had commented sarcastically when the hand was over.

The Chairman sighed. How to construct an address from all of these thoughts? Abandoning his cold cocoa, he went to the fridge, poured himself a glass of white wine, then settled down at his keyboard again.

to be continued...